The Present Tense

The Present Tense Allen Road South: Annus Mirabilis

Poems by Don Mager

No part of this work may be reproduced or transmitted in any form or by any means, electronic or mechanical, including by photocopying or recording, or by any information storage or retrieval system without the proper written permission of the copyright owner unless such copying is expressly permitted by federal copyright law. Thurston Howl Publications is authorized to grant permission for further uses of the work in this book. Permission must be obtained by the author or the publication house. Address requests for permission to make copies of material here to the email address jonathan.thurstonhowlpub@gmail.com

ISBN: 978-1-945247-34-7

THE PRESENT TENSE

Copyright © 2013 Don Mager

First Edition, 2018. All rights reserved.

A Thurston Howl Publications Book

Published by Thurston Howl Publications
thurstonhowlpublications.com
Lansing, MI

Edited by Starshield Lortie

jonathan.thurstonhowlpub@gmail.com

Printed in the United States of America
10 9 8 7 6 5 4 3 2 1

This book is for Bill and our family:
Marlowe and Megan,
Rainer, Sachiko, Saniko Jenny, and Yukiko Becky
And Javon Terah, Eugenia, Shamar, Cwesei, and Kedan

Life has not just taken place. Art never just began. It has been constantly taking place before it manifested itself.

It is infinite. And here, in this moment for me and in me, it is—as if from a suddenly opened up assembly hall, pouring out to scald me with fresh headlong universality and sempiternity, it, this moment: is the result of a promise.

No true book has a first page. Like the sounds of a forest, its utterance God knows from where grows and flows, awaking secrets of the wilderness, and then suddenly, during the darkest, most stunning and panicked moment, starts, having arrived, conversing with all the tree tops.

Boris Pasternak. "Some Principles," No.4 (1918-9)

Even lost in dreaming, poetry encounters nature. The living, verifiable world is the only enterprise of the imagination that has ever succeeded and continues still to succeed. Right here it continues successfully in its moment-by-moment newness. Still, entirely—it is verifiable, deep, continuously engrossing, and in no way disappointing on the morning after. It sets the example for the poet to a greater degree than does a model painted from life.

Boris Pasternak. "Some Principles," from No.6 (1918-9)

Жизнь пошла не сейчас. Искусство никогда не начиналось. Оно бывало постоянно налицо до того, как становилось. Оно бесконечно. И здесь, в этот миг за мной и во мне, оно --- таково, что из внезапно раскрывшегося актового зала меня обдает его свежей и стремительной повсеместностью и повсевременностью, будто это: приводят мгновение к присяге.

Ни у какой истинной книге нет первой страницы. Как лесной шум, она зарождается Бог весть где, и растет, и катится, будя заповедные дебри, и вдруг, в самый темный, ошеломительный и панический миг, заговаривает всеми вершинами сразу, докатившись.

Бортис Пастернак. «Несколько положений.» Собрание Сочинений в Пяти Томах. Москва: Художественная литература, 1989-1991. Том 4.368.

Фантазируя, наталкивается поэзия на природу. Живой, действительный мир --- это единственный, однажды удавшийся и все еще без конца удачный замысел воображения. Вот он длится, ежемгновенно успешный. Он все еще --- действителен, глубок, неотрывно увлекателен, в нем не разочаровываешься на другое утро. Он служит поэту примером в большей еще степени, нежели --- натурой и моделью

Пастернак, Борис Леонидович.

Пастернак. «Несколько положений.» Том 4.369-370.

Preface

Starting with my first chapbook *To Track The Wended One* (1986), several of my books are projects built on a concept: *Glosses, Borderings, Good Turns, Birth Daybook, Drive Time* and *Russian Riffs*. I like to think of each as an assignment I gave myself. *The Present Tense* is my biggest assignment. I was awed by Boris Pasternak's revolutionary early book *My Sister — Life,* in the incomparable translations of Mark Rudman and Bohdan Boychuk, and Pasternak's aesthetic 1918 statements in "Some Principles" from the Russian Edition of Paternak's Complete Works. I was forcefully challenged by the two of his principals, which I call injunctions. Through him I realized most poetry describes the actual world (nature, weather, etc.) as typicalities and generalities, not as specificities. We get descriptions of sunrises or storms, not a sunrise nor a storm. Pasternak's "injunctions" led me to this assignment from which *The Present Tense* took shape. My assignment had four prompts:

1. Write one poem for each day of entire year and do so on a daily basis.

2. Write every poem exclusively in the present tense — "This now." No past and no future. When there is a slight shift of time, it is in terms of how as the observer in his now observes that now's slight shift.

3. Write about the now observed not abut the observer. The observer/speaker/poet is never referenced with personal pronouns.

4. To capture the surprise of specificity as charged by Pasternak's "Principles," I learned from the synesthesia which makes his early books so remarkable. I evoke all five senses (as well as kinesthesia), often exploiting a Paternakean synesthetic "shock" of describing one sense in terms of another.

The four prompts together serve Pasternak's injunction to reveals a *"living, verifiable world...in its moment-by-moment newness."*

An additional part of my assignment entails form. I have dallied with the sonnet form in many ways over the years. *The Present Tense* poems are all in unrhymed syllabic sonnets. The nine syllable lines avoid the repetitiveness of an iambic beat. The line breaks allow for surprising, even awkward, enjoyments as well the gratification closures with line-end periods. Syllabic disruption of meter, surprise, awkwardness and end-stop gratifications within the containment of a set form also serve Pasternak's injunction

January Journal

1
Tuesday, January 1, 2013

Morning's head-throb hangs over in a
cloud's low uninflected monochrome.
Threatening to break into clarity
of snow, it wears night's nausea in its
stomach pit. Even though the windows
glance out now and again with hesitant
expectancy, the break does not break.
Look, the window says, *noon glides down a*
street that still has rings of streetlight light
pooled on its pavement. A dog sniffs trash
at the curb and dodges car beams. Her
sag of stretched nipples flaps beneath her
ribs. Like a tattered oily rag, her
cold tail skulks between her trembling legs.

2
Wednesday, January 2, 2013

The nightfall snow wakes up the woods with
white carpets and dripping branches. It
prances dog paw prints in crisscross rings
that trail around the trees. Water coughs
and gurgles in streamlets melting out
between the frosted drifts of leaves. Sky's
blue sings a child's birthday picnic
in a park. From the trees, ice-melts sing
of wind chimes. The puppy's song plunges
into a small drift and rolls about.
Leaping up, it's a shimmy rumba.
Its torso spits a cold fine shower of
light glints through welcoming air. Soggy
socks glow on the warmth of trudging feet.

The Present Tense

3
Thursday, January 3, 2013

Wind stiffens its resolve and by noon
its unpremeditated punches
snap off high death-throe limbs. Like brittle
snapping bones, they crack out loud and sprawl
in helpless freefall to the damp ivy
carpet below. They shatter. As wind turns
its mind the other way, it raises
small sharp hackles and looks up. Sheet on
sheet of granite gray cloud layers in
and weighs its mounting weight down. Cloud meets
the wind, eye to eye. They embrace in
instant kindred recognition. They
swear allegiance to pal around for
the rest of the afternoon. And do.

4
Friday, January 4, 2013

Out front, dawn slowly climbs from its dinge
gray eiderdown of clouds. This side, bright
with floodlight, the track to the compost
bin in the far back yard trudges through
ivy crystallized with crisp frost. Each
rubber-thong-and-sock print crushes the
silver glaze with its rude weight. Holding
savor on the tongue like chilled Chablis, breath
inhales ice's tang. Like a groggy
child, dawn dawdles in its gray snug sky.
It procrastinates and pouts with
weak excuses. It stalls plans to streak
frosty roofs with mica schists of light.
Back inside socks are clammy and cold.

5
Saturday, January 5, 2013

The slim debilitated moon cuts
a slow blade through damp air hung from sky's
dark underside. Ground fog hangs from low
branches to creep flat swathes around blind
bends in the road. Sporadic chucking
sounds of male Possums on the prowl hang
blind enigmas in log rot thickets.
Like wraiths frozen in black holes of time,
backyard lights hang inside small glowing
clouds. Glinting a pale white, the feeble
flutter of a moth hangs in the web
stretched like gauze from bulb to steel pole. In
suspended animation, dawn hangs
just on the edge of the turning earth.

6
Sunday, January 6, 2013

Beneath the high sky's cathedral vault
of glow, cold night hunkers down over
the city as still as any stone.
It squats on silent buttocks, a large
grotesque and voiceless gargoyle. The earth
is frozen like pond ice on which, with
heads tucked in folds of motionless wings,
the flock of ducks huddles—as still as
any stone. Quietness settles in
so hard that it fails to hear the train's
painful moan. Like a cat on the prowl,
the moan slips beside dark warehouses
and bright parking lots in their gapping
emptiness. It leaves no trace at all.

7
Monday, January 7, 2013

As light seamlessly drifts into dusk,
sky's libation arms reach to earth with
the flowing down of spaciousness. Space
fills voids between stark unmoving trees.
It overflows between them stretching
distance out to the horizon's white
light. It bestows its armful of
stillness over earth's cold face. Earth looks
up. The cleanse of light washes over.
Like down comforters tugged snug up to
dream-destined eyes, the drowsy shadows
thicken. Glinting weakly in their small
loneliness, horizon-hugging
yard lights a half-mile away come on.

8
Tuesday, January 8, 2013

Crow casuistries split hairs over
the fine points of entrails and torn
flesh. Between shreds and guzzled morsels,
their three-way debate about the splattered
Raccoon drags on and on. To avoid
more smear of bloodshed, cars headed to
work, jerk and veer. No need to worry.
With timing as tight as acrobats,
shaving the air from the oncoming
grille, the crows' splashing wings flap up. The
car slips past. Three sprawling flaps down, they're
back. Squabbling proceeds. No agreement
in sight. The neighborhood stands by as
witness—too prudent to intervene.

9
Wednesday, January 9, 2013

From the horizon's edges, flowing
out beneath the cold roof of low clouds,
light spreads its cautionary tale. With
every glance and stare, it urges, *to
name is to tame.* Blushes whispering
from dead clay and dry lawn may say they're
green. This is their temporary fix.
Refusing to let go, Hornbeam leaves
say: *call us maybe amber, maybe
copper, we'll wait here tomorrow.* With
patient resignation, light wears the
yellowed afternoon's pale glow while a
squirrel flicks his tail. As dark closes
in, his tasks are his full attention.

10
Thursday, January 10, 2013

Defiant in their clinging dry leaves,
aureoles of Hornbeam trees float in
a coppery glow. Backyard barren
trunks of Sycamores and Oaks and Elms
stand black in their widowed procession
up the hill and out to the wooded
stoic dusk's afterglow. Spaced apart
in randomness, like ballerinas
frozen in silence on the edge of night's
curtain fall, the glowing trees—half the
height or less of their mourning sisters—
balance on the toe-point of gold-tinged
stationary time. Neither curtain
nor applause, the dark's embrace is stealth.

11
Friday, January 11, 2013

Dawn lines the horizon with mold-grown
slate tiles. It rears shapeless drapes. Atop
the spindly poles of damp clammy trees,
it lowers a musty canvas tent
of uninspired clouds. Finishing
its dreary labor, it settles down
to out-wait day's force of sun. Sun shrinks
to a plate and creeps behind the dinge
of drapes. In their drab bed of sour mulch,
as if they'd lost their last shred of cheer,
shy iris ears prick up. Leaf-scattered
porches wheeze asthmatic breaths. Dawn's eyes
squint and smart from nightlong residues
of fireplace smoke. Its defiance wins.

12
Saturday, January 12, 2013

The deck chair decides to share its mug
of steamy black tea with the noon sky.
The sky is fast-forward gyrating
bundles of white Hydrangeas. They mass
together. They sweep high up the blue
horizons. Like boats on swelling tides
adrift, they break apart and bump each
other about. Interstices of
warm sun cascade through the sporadic
blue gaps. The tea mug's face leans back to
take gulps of slapping sun and dashes
of sudden cloudy chill. Trade-offs of heat
and cold lull eyes closed. The half-full mug
splashes with a thud to the wood floor.

13
Sunday, January 13, 2013

As small lakes tuck small secrets in wood-
land pockets behind the backyard gate
and beyond the road where, in faded
paint, a *LOTS FOR SALE* sign stands, morning's
sun draws bold shadows. They underline
the barrenness of trees. In place of
warmth they offer sturdy alibis.
Five black ducks lift above the rear
view tree line. During their short commute,
rasps sputter like bassoons. Their shadows
drift portents darkly across the yard.
They settle their secrets down on the
pond across the road. Without comment,
five ducks—five shadows—swim side by side.

14
Monday, January 14, 2013

With its open eye, moon watches the
calligraphy of Hawks sketched across
the clean sky. One—a pair—now all at
once, six—arc and float. The atmosphere
ambushes upturned hand-shaded eyes
with disbelieving amazement of
Robin eggshell—everywhere. Touching
each compass point and mid-day hour, blue
goes on and on and on. The languor
of Hawk flight belies its urgency
of hungry time. As shadowed eyes and
upturned palm welcome evanescence
in the air, the moon's far orbit rides
pallid inattentive apathy.

15
Tuesday, January 15, 2013

Drab holly leaves prick silver sequins
from the tips—streaming in volleys through
tall bare trees—of spear shaft light. Nursing
its clutches of brittle green pretenses
as they wait to turn pomegranate
red, the leaves wear their stoic winter
green. Sunlight tirelessly darts
silver foil on the windshield frost. It stabs
school bus drivers' eyes. Sashaying
like a torn rag from the fresh sky, a Blue
Jay's spread wings swoop the holly's low branch.
A second torn shred darts behind. Between
the dark green leaves, their fleet blue scotch and
hop game parries with rust dagger shrieks.

16
Wednesday, January 16, 2013

The abrupt plume of violet-gray
clouds bullies the midday sun. Through air's
breathless stillness, sudden menace drops
chilly ripples on arms and down napes.
Its *volta-faca* turn skids the day
around. Sleet slings down relentless
bridal rice. Sidewalks cracks fill up with
neat white lines. Lawn's disordered shag-grass
rug mottles a maze of white and chaff.
Having a good laugh at its punch line
prank, the cloud packs up and rushes east.
Light bursts from hiding. As sleet wilts to
fading memories, napes and arms lap
up the sunshine's eager puppy licks.

17
Thursday, January 17, 2013

Daffodil bulbs hold up their small green
distaffs promising, in good time, spun
gold. Hectoring today's now, they say:
*So winter damp will soak its fecund
scent deep, compost your veggie beds now.*
But the arctic fringe, driving its jet
deep south, in a few stern gusts, sweeps in.
It wipes off the smile of that advice
with a single brisk slap. Riding the
wings of dusk, over porch-steps, cars and
streets, and landing as ice, its sloppy
breath drools. Along gutters, from house to
house, icicles string glass necklaces.
As street lights wink on, their facets gleam.

18
Friday, January 18, 2013

Dawn's smoothness spreads its dark contralto
satin from road shoulder to shoulder.
Its soprano silk lilts a silver
vocalise on car windows staring
out from driveways. Still snuggled under
shadows, sidewalks and brick porch-steps
mask surreptitious treacheries.
The front door sneaks a peek out, retreats
and chooses prudence. The pair of Doves
chooses instead to flutter down through
the gray light. They tandem-bob and pick
old seeds from the frosty grass. Dawn seeps
through to streak copper-tan glisters from
tail to head on each bird's stately back.

The Present Tense

19
Saturday, January 19, 2013

Air empties itself of everything
but dryness and the afternoon's harsh
glare. Its grip empties out any shred
of dust and motion. Breeze has errands
elsewhere and leaves air derelict. Like
a solitary limestone outcrop,
it hangs alone in its undisturbed
silence. Its light is vacuous of
warmth—its silence, vacuous of birds—
and traffic—and house doors slamming shut.
Absence contains and fills its presence.
Its void is shapely—its null, new. Like
breath, it draws in deeply, and, grandly,
flows back out. In. Out. In. Breath—air—one.

20
Sunday, January 20, 2013

Not loosening its skillful grip, hand
over hand, across afternoon's high
wire, the warm dry air's September cache
of memories holds as steady as
the cat crouched beneath crumpled Pampas
Grass fixated, without a twitch, on
the pecking Chickadee. Like clockwork,
warmth works its way from noon to the ebb
of the sun. Abruptly sunset's
chill slashes day from night. It drops the
bottom right out. Its cymbal smacks at
ears. Its whip lashes eyes. It is the
dark conundrum that calls for heavy
frost before dawn. Its will will be done.

21
Monday, January 21, 2013

Assuming cars have neither haste nor
destinations, the congregation
of assembled geese meanders, one
plodding pigeon-toed web-foot after
the next, across the intersection.
The intersection holds its noon hour
rush of breath and cancels plans for quick-
stop errands on the way. As slow as
methodical drips from a shower
head, the geese feet march to a different
beat. Grass sprigs and Wild Onion tufts in
sun bright lawns are their calculus of
time and destination. Noon follows
suit while the intersection unclogs.

22
Tuesday, January 22, 2013

Too faint to see, the glasses' fogging,
early morning mist limps past. Its charm
is empty. On its shoulders, it wears
clouds' large dark threatenings. Their unfulfilled
taunts of rain collapse. They punctuate
with impatient whipping gusts of wind.
Dust devils dance up the gravel drive
and shrink back. Miniature tornadoes
swirl dry leaves across the yard. From
opposing edges of the sky, weak
thunder blusters. Bubbling through the clouds
off and on all morning getting no-
where, skittery flashes of light rant.
Windshield mist's a long-forgotten tease.

23
Wednesday, January 23, 2013

The sky's rare and imperious black
diamond overflows from brim to brim.
Flawless icy air burnishes off
drifts of chimney smoke and slips of cloud.
Bare branches part like arms, opened to
exhale breath from lung pits up and out
into the cosmos. Facets pierce and
burn. Like a white clover meadow, suns,
galaxies and nebulae convene in
the eye's numberless democracy.
With the exhaled breath, they tug the neck
backwards to the edge of a cramp to
cradle and hold a brimful, almost
excruciating, extreme of gaze.

24
Thursday, January 24, 2013

Driveways have sent their cars off to work.
Sun washes warmth and frost out from the
late morning air. Solitary and
still it stands in its starch. Pale greens bleach
out from grass stubble in the lawn. Weed
straw is overhung with Cornflower
stalks. Beside the culvert beneath the
road, Pampas Grass sweeps broken feather
dusters down over the dank clay of
the creek bank. Motionlessness stands full
and statuesque beside its cousin
timelessness. As the sun drags its slow
white girth across the milky southern
sky, their abundance fills up the air.

25
Friday, January 25, 2013

Dawn fog spreads a muffled pall over
intermittent street light pools and dank
shapeless shadows. Beneath the shroud, the
dying Possum lies. Where the car tire
hit and knocked it from the street, it gasps
in the leaf-rot. Its teeth-spiky snout
pulses shut and open. Each pulse faintly
squawks. The tail's leathery pink stretches
out in murky light. The puddle of
brackish blood swells. In the dawn's slow now
the Possum fades into weaker and
weaker chirps until the serrations
of its teeth gape in a pulseless snout—
awakened into frozen silence.

26
Saturday, January 26, 2013

Late night drivers return to ice-glazed
walkways and porch steps. Air tastes garlic
raw—and cruel like exposed buried bones.
Wind blows cayenne puffs of Canada
breath. It sears eyes and scalds cheeks. Its tongue
wraps numbing knots on finger joints. It
fumbles keys. They crash down the cement
porch steps like broken china. The moon's
spotlight spots them. There they are. There's the
knob, the key slot. The door falls open.
Securely banished, the brute force of
now's dark interrogations is shut
out, while up-stream, with no earthly care,
the moon's full-face brightness orbits on.

The Present Tense

27
Sunday, January 27, 2013

As small taunts of stingy snow leave no
memory, the drought digs into cold
clay-red soil like bricks. Its long-trekking
camel tongue laps the spindly trickle
in the stream. Like figs and dates, sun-dried
and hard, it dehydrates underbrush
that lies in wait for any spark or
butt to make fury howl. The stiffened
ice wind consorts to help cut furrows
in the brow and slender creases in
backs of hands. It cracks inner nostrils
and draws faint blood-pink smears. Impervious
to evening, noon or dawn, drought's present
tense trudges on with bludgeoned feet.

28
Monday, January 28, 2013

The creek's bank-side shows its age-dry skin.
Where the dead grass's hair thins, clay cracks
with crow's feet creases. Some spots are as
still and bald as any stone. Exposed
like eviscerated nerves, dangling
above the creek bed's trickle of slow
dementia, roots hang. Arthritic gnarls
of ankle-thick Wisteria vines
cling desperately to tree trunks. Like an
old friend making its daily visit
to the hospice, the dutiful
sun drags its cold shoulder across the
morning sky. The creek looks up and asks:
Is that you, old fella'? Here again?

29
Tuesday, January 29, 2013

Leaf mulch and dead grass welcome the light's slant
pouring through spider-branches. Shadows
cut dark lines. Too busy to keep count,
Chickadees zip in and out of the
early afternoon chill. From a fence
post, one repeats its tin fife, four note,
minor descending scale. Others rake
through the dry lawn. The blond feral cat,
sun warmed, lolls on the deck. Its drowsy
eyelids contemplate a prowl. Its tail
twitches. Its leap waits to slink along
the wall's shade. Afternoon holds a deep
yoga inhalation of white and
photographic black serenity.

30
Wednesday, January 30, 2013

Peripatetic slow gyroscopes
shift the ice white stars. Sky's dome turns from
black to even blacker predawn black.
Robed and slippered with hands pulled inside
sleeves, the dreamer escapes his groggy
dream. The deck chair holds vigil as the
peripatetic swirl of image
and incoherence fades. One by one,
each uncertainty becomes a point
of diamond clarity. Knowing it's
watched, the sky explains: *See, each star finds
another—then another. Blackness
has no end of lights to find.* The chair
grows cold. Slippers shuffle back to bed.

31
Thursday, January 31, 2013

The sun's breathless lava blaze sings an
aubade to longings for the night to
disappear into the clarity
of morning's bracingly crisp hello.
Eager to get on with the job at
hand, it climbs over the threshold edge
of earth and spreads its vast hibiscus
bloom between the silhouetted trees.
As its scarlet face balances just
above the tree line pausing to catch
its breath before mounting the white sky,
the bus stop's squinted eyes cannot tear
away. With gloved hands fending blindness
and welling tears, gazers simply gaze.

February Journal

32
Friday, February 1, 2013

The breeze is scuffing around, listless
with nudges and abrupt stern gusts. It
racks the porch roof with the old oak's small
cache of forlorn acorns. Its doldrums
sweep small dried leaf eddies up the street
to park beneath parked cars. Large cloud starched
islands skiff armadas across the
sun. Abruptly cutting off straight-edge
light shafts on the kitchen walls, shadows skiff
ominously across the windows.
On no premeditated schedule,
all afternoon wind knocks the wind chimes
to announce it's going nowhere soon.
All afternoon shadows raise and close.

33
Saturday, February 2, 2013

Silent doldrums of sharp air sting the
morning's face. Attenuated clouds
drape the sky. The white sun turns a cold
shoulder. Birds settle differences and
share the bare yard. They sort through dried leaves,
dried grass, scruffy weeds. Wrens. Chickadees.
Sparrows. Robins. Jays. Seeds as small as
midges are the menu. On an oak
trunk above their busy conclave, a
lone Woodpecker hopes to turn up a
few odd ants in the aloof bark cracks.
Along the sidewalk, as if out for
a weekend stroll, Pansies lift yellow
and lavender Pekingese faces.

34
Sunday, February 3, 2013

Rime frost whispers diamonds along the
wild Rhododendron leaves as they stand
in solo eagerness above the
wetland muck and underbrush. Sunlight
cascades over distant warehouse roofs
along the tracks setting alight the leaves'
chandeliers. They flare silently in
silver facets of clinking crystal.
Their silence calls out to the raucous
duck flock paddling across the low
sky like beginning swimmers. Blinds
drawn wide, the window can't take back its
astonishment. It simply lets the
coffee mug's steam exhale as it cools.

35
Monday, February 4, 2013

Intermittent wipers clear fine-mesh
rain from homebound evening windshields. Clouds
press foamy fog down across barren
tree lines. Fireplace smoke sputters up from
chimneys. Too weak to push away the
clouds, it folds back across the roofs. It swings
piquant incense censers down across
driveways. It breathes toasted cedar scent
into gaping mouths of raised trunk lids
and deposits light residues on
damp haired drivers unloading grocery
bags. The low clouds lock arms in a closed
circle to block the enervated
sun. Frigid rain stiffens its resolve.

36
Tuesday, February 5, 2013

Sly with ice, beneath satin shrouds, the
predawn roads lurk. They want sun to lie
low. They want clouds to hug thick mittens
across the tops of trees. They want fog
to blow egg-white froth into squinting
eyes of headlights. Dustings of powdered
sugar sweeten sidewalk treacheries.
Hardened glazes seal cold inside locked
car doors and keyholes. When dawn's small gray
pokes out to sniff the air before its
caution creeps from the horizon, roads,
sidewalks, blind lights and key slots, frozen
in time and poised to snap, join forces
conspiring to hide skids, spins and falls.

37
Wednesday, February 6, 2013

Sky's flattened cloudless platter slides its
short hour into the chromatic scale
of yellow's pitches. Overhead spreads
creamy buttermilk. Lower west, it
edges toward pineapple. Then lemon.
Turmeric. As it slips away, its
eyes too piercing to smile, the half sun
glows. Against the cold, sky holds still in
its golden Beryl moment. It cracks
as vapor trails appear and spread. One
lifts from the airport at the city's
far other side. The other streams down.
Their undersides burn. Rise of crimson
aims straight toward magenta's steep descent.

38
Thursday, February 7, 2013

Reflected light pales the dome of cloud. The
lower edges search for lost horizons
behind the predawn woods. Earth exhales
swaths of smoke-drift fog. Horizons can't
be found. Backed by gray haze, woodland trees—
across the street—out behind the gate—wave
straight stark trunks and black boney branches.
Like agitated kelp forests in
slow milky gray currents, they sway their
unsynchronized upturned pendulums.
Bare legs in rubber thongs crouch over
bushes to find the morning news. Its
paper's damp. Predawn reports its news:
restlessness, dank gray and heavy dew.

39
Friday, February 8, 2013

Noon's methodical stillness shoots sun's
cold glare through stiff bare trees. They straddle
their embarrassed dwarfish shadows. Flat
light spreads evenly across vine snarls,
leaf beds and log rot. It douses dried
grass in backyard lawns. The hour holds
a statuesque pose. It would like to
glance away and not look back. No breeze
fusses with the amber parchment of
Hornbeam leaves. Looking back, the hour has
no time to hold a pose. The holly's
ruby bangles tremble. Cardinals hop
from sprig to sprig. Their plucky shadows
on the bare earth below join their feast.

40
Saturday, February 9, 2013

Thudding about in cold bare trees, night's
undertows to rising—ebbing—dreams
beach their flotsam and jetsam beneath
dark midmorning clouds. Shipwreck beams from
tall masts of old oaks splash the soggy
yard. Rotted chunks of pith, slabs of bark
like blown off shingles, branches spiked with
white barbs of lichen strew the brash wind's
debris. The back-humped wheelbarrow
ferries the long yard, load on load. Noon
piles up its curbside pickup mound. Its
damp rot spreads through the clammy air. The
bent back unkinks in its sweat chilled shirt.
Sun drifts its pale spot behind the clouds.

41
Sunday, February 10, 2013

With neither herald nor fanfare, at
the edge of the ear's full attention,
mid-morning's hush sidles down the street
from both ends and takes possession. Frost
fully thaws and leaves hushed droplets on
the lawn's dry grass. Utility trucks,
ladders hung to their sides, rattle past
and leave hushed pavement in their oily
exhaust. The haze, blurring the inner
sanctum of druidic woods across
the road, clears, showing the hush of an
imagined conclave. Casting out and
reeling in, ear imagines nothing.
It hears this now now. Hush mimes its song.

42
Monday, February 11, 2013

The sun slips off its ledge, banishing
clouds and vapor trails in a regal
hand wave. The western sky dilutes its
lurid palette with milks and creams. It
puts roadway minds and hillside window
eyes to rest. Scarlet thins to champagne
peach. Rambunctious orange and tangerine
are tamed. Their soft coral glows. And where
imperial purple strives for full
dominion, a melt of lilac, mauve
and gray usurps the throne. Night decides
time is right to take things easy and
grants the fading light, reprieve. Long-held
frost-chilled breaths exhale and draw back in.

43
Tuesday, February 12, 2013

The clouds crack apart and the sun's bright
puddles trickle down, on and off all
afternoon like a tip-toe toddler
messing with the switch. The seductive
scentless scents of daffodils lick spots
of time lit by spots of light. They tug
at nose with silence and in return
nose drinks in absence as if they were
another face that certainty
wears. They call neither butterflies nor
bees. Their allure beckons only eyes.
Their consummation is this now's now
whose purpose is simply to be an
almost purposeless festivity.

44
Wednesday, February 13, 2013

Dogs are walked. Sweat-shirted joggers, brisk
and showered, are on their way to work.
Now, morning's pause awaits the conductor's
raised baton to silence the coughs and
shuffling in seats. The trash truck trundles
up. Its thumb clutch heaves curbside bins like
trembling babies dandled overhead
and sets them back. It moves on down the
street. Commotion's residue settles
back in icy anticipation.
With a forecast as certain as a
timpani roll or pigeon flurry
of violins scampering down and
up their strings, street's held-breath waits for snow.

45
Thursday, February 14, 2013

The overnight snowfall welcomes ice
water drips from branch thaw and high wire
icicles. Beneath streetlight circles
the shallow snow glows as if on spaced
out banquet tables. The drippings cut
patterns on the predawn tablecloths.
The fresh starched white of now's breakfast guest
anticipation turns inside out
into the apprehensive now of
traffic's slush. Beneath the overhang
of a dribbling tree, flip-flops and socks
stand at the driveway end. The pristine
lace circles of white assure them, yes,
morning's paper, of course, runs late.

46
Friday, February 15, 2013

With recorder dulcet chords, eastern
light unfurls modulations. Sky-blue
pink blends seamless creamy sherbet hues
of blue with pink and hues of pink with
blue. Light mounts—unbearable in its
seamless lightness of being—here—dawn—
now. As white as a crashing Russian
meteor flash, vapor-trail streaks draw
bars and crosses on the pastel wash.
Destinies and destinations ride
their trails. Ice white traces unfurl their
separate days. For now they are as safe
and silent as a fading lip print
on a watching breath-steamed window pane.

47
Saturday, February 16, 2013

As earth's face stops to look back across
its shoulder, light swells up from beneath the
tree lined black horizon. Light carves cloud
striations with watercolor brush
stroke pigments—fluent and dried. It drives its
rippling ribs across the Saharan
expanse of sky dunes: yellow, copper,
cream and aquamarine. Wind has no
hand in the sky's pose of timelessness.
Rolling up its cold black hump, earth's face
turns back to follow the sun down. In
its wake, light ripples certainty
of dimness. With expanding swathes of
dark, charcoal washes fill the clouds in.

48
Sunday, February 17, 2013

Night inherits evening's unperturbed
bequest of slow wet snow. Contrary
to the all-night drip and slush customs
of these climes, it revives the ways of
bygone years and holds this sudden fleece
close unto the now of its cold heart.
Its entirety of refracted
luminescence glows across the trees
and roofs. Unperturbed degrees sink and,
like a frozen whipped coconut and
egg-white cream dessert, snow sets hard. Night's
big convexity of sky glows with
Abalone's inner pinkish pearl.
Obsidian hard streets shine black back.

49
Monday, February 18, 2013

Chunks crash from branches and sweat into
the ground. Icicles drip until their
hollowed fragility cracks and clatters
to the sidewalk. From its cloudless tall
Aegean sky, midmorning sun scans
the wide expanse of thaw and wet. Only
north side shadows of thick trunks lurk with
small pools of snow in the red mulch bark.
The sun's present tense has no time for
memory or regret. Night's fleece of
white is its amnesia. Evening's
dried out lawn and street are not yet wish—
nor threat. With drip—crash—clatter—now is
morning's liquefying quickstep dance.

50
Tuesday, February 19, 2013

Midmorning moves the tree trunk shadows
to sweep off the last of the frost. The
bleach blond lawn and mower mulch return
the favor. They scatter Chickadees
in bobbling swathes and watch for the swoop
of mettlesome Jays. The twitching lawn
bares its chest to pricking beaks that pick
up seeds and pitch leaves behind their backs.
The unblinking blue glass eye holds the
sky's fixed gaze as it sheds a pair of
bully Jays to pounce on the flock's midst.
Pretending to be alarmed, the lawn
scuffs up a hasty flutter of wings,
then settles right back into business.

51
Wednesday, February 20, 2013

From edge to ripened edge, evening shakes
out and spreads its peach skin sheet across
the sky. Dulcet flannel fuzz summons
eyes to nuzzle in its fur as if
they were soft kittens. It calls ears to
hear its unsung serenata of
farewell. The snowy trees and house roofs
stand in a stark brief parenthesis
of stillness. The evening's somnolent
barcarole attains its mooring and
disembarks. First here, then over there,
then imperceptibly, lights prick through
everywhere onto precipitous
night's teeming star wakened piazza.

52
Thursday, February 21, 2013

Like headless Harlequin legs on stilts,
trees along the fence line up in green
pantaloons of shimmering ivy.
As if to drive off the sun bright cold,
wind's vivacious quickstep goads them on.
Like twinkling emeralds, sun jingles mute
tiny ivy bells down and up their
pants. In leaps from tree to tree and zig-
zag hurtles across the ivy floor,
a squirrel Pierrot pursues his nimble
Columbine. The puppet master sun
mottles the spectacle with fitful
spotlights and ominous shadow blots.
Wind's cold applause clamors for encores.

53
Friday, February 22, 2013

As morning ebbs down to puddles in
slippery dead grass where sunlight lays
broad bands between the cold shadows that
stretch out from sheds and houses, it grubs
about on orange geese feet tugging up
sprigs of Wild Garlic and fragile grass
and plopping down white splats of guano.
It waddles along from snaking neck
to fluffed-up tail. Content inside its small
attention and methodical as a
wind-up toy, this now plods right along.
While shadow bands and sun bands link their
arms in chilly camaraderie,
the hour only haggles over haste.

54
Saturday, February 23, 2013

Morning entices the giddy sun
to caress and sway like clothes drying
on a line. Across the neighbor's yard
from hedge to Junipers, song Sparrows
inundate the placid float of time
with florid interrogations and
replies. Oblivious Robins cock
their ears at patches of fresh mown grass.
A Blue Jay's threat fizzles. He retreats
to the pear's low branch. Rapt in high-wire
daydreams, a Dove pair coos. Enticing
feet to test skin against the deck's stain
of satin wood, warmth's seamless tai chi
grace modulates to the key of noon.

55
Sunday, February 24, 2013

The pavilion tent of taut stretched clouds
holds down the city's glow of lights.
The glow sifts silver silken mist through
starkly barren trees to scatter a
mottle of breadcrumb pebbles along the
backyard path. Hooded sweater and work
boots trace the path with fairy footsteps
and puffs of gauzy breath. The bare porch
bulb dims to an echo of its beam.
The far gate leads the path out into
the woods' stretch of black trunks until the
fading of a distant owl's hollow call
transforms stillness into an even stiller
echo of itself.
                It calls again.

56
Monday, February 25, 2013

Beyond the fresh homebound slush and mud,
past sidewalks splotched with ice puddles and
thaw spots, backyards stretch toward the sinking
sun. It draws long gray-fuchsia shadows
in elegant parallels across
the fragile flannel of glowing snow.
The random lace of Chickadee prints
and squirrel tracks is pricked out in this
pristine quiet and the tall bare trees
nestle this quiet in their dark clumps
of Mistletoe and up and down their
ivy ropes of malachite. Now is
this quiet, as seamless purple fills
the shadows; and quiet is this now.

57
Tuesday, February 26, 2013

On its dog leash of refusal, feet
anchored in the young bright grass shoots and
wet clay, the drizzle persists in its
standoff with the afternoon—the whole
afternoon. Settled in, it delights
in squirrels' tireless mating chases as
they flash down and up trees to fly through
wet space and swing on dripping branches.
The branches shiver and swerve. Drizzle's
laconic smile watches the sun's dim
ride behind slate gray walls. As char black
soaks it up, the low sky takes no note
and drizzle snuggles in for the night.
Night's wide maternal arms wrap it round.

58
Wednesday, February 27, 2013

Red throat stretched to the horizontal
slant of late day light, the Robin sits
on the Sycamore branch's graying
silhouette. The stream glugs thaw water
far below. Fluffed in her winter fur,
a nearby rabbit chews small evening
grass. Hawks recede from long afternoon
prowls. Scolding back and forth, they decamp
to their half-dead oak tree nest. Early
night exhales puffs of frosty air. Perched
in cavalier disregard, the red
throat spills variegated streams of high-
pitched glitter. Spot-lit by fading beams,
his red breast's now swells full stage center.

59
Thursday, February 28, 2013

Lunchtime clouds conspire together for
a sneak attack. Alarmed car windows
battle to see through waves abruptly splashed
across them as oncoming lights smear
and blind. Downspouts gag with clots of leaves.
Geysers spew faucets out from roofs. Curb
drains choke and, spanning intersections,
back-flow into rivers. Total rout.
The clouds' campaign brings grand success.
With injury on insult, their secret
weapon cuts ice pick stabs on faces,
backs of necks and ungloved hands, while claps
and thunder-rumbles unzip the sky
in a bombardment of fireworks.

March Journal

60
Friday, March 1, 2013

Swelling clouds dim the midnight sky. Ash
oozes to charcoal. Charcoal oozes
to slate and etches the ridge of bare
trees and spindly cedars. Their branches
are as motionless as any stone.
They are a frieze of black puppet sticks.
They are black construction paper cut-
out silhouettes. They are torn patches
of unraveling old black lace. Their
breezeless owl-less silence expects both
cold drizzly rain and its failure to
arrive. Unable to tell which is
which, porch light's flick looks out at faintly
damp porch steps. Abruptly it flicks off.

61
Saturday, March 2, 2013

Rain's small icy needles drive straight down
in voile curtains. Behind one wide
sheet lies the opaque sheet of another.
Behind it another. They vanish
at a distance that has no point to
vanish in. Without sun to shift the
dial hands, low clouds soak time into
sponges and wring out droplets of noon
mixed with morning and afternoon mixed
into a pretend sunless sunset.
Tear-drop diamonds in neat strands along
undersides of twigs forge themselves into
pretend iceless glints. Grass-clay sponges
soak the air in and wring nothing out.

62
Sunday, March 3, 2013

The long spindle shafts of morning sun
spin gold from distaffs of the stiff green
daffodils. The buds pop open like
tissues of paper origami
party favors. Theirs is the sash's
gold of flower girls toddling up the
aisle in white crabapple flounces—the
butter gold whipped stiff from churning cream.
Like kindred souls, blossoms stare into
the sun's huge retina. Its silent
sling-shot gaze stares back. As sun floats up
the southern buttressed arch of sky, in
reply, the daffodils pivot their
well-oiled, full-arc necks—like dwarf owls.

63
Monday, March 4, 2013

Late morning oversees the mower's
aftermath. Wild Garlic spikes the air.
Beheaded Dandelions strew small
shreds of yellow tissue across swathes
of drying fresh shorn grass. Beyond the
hedge, crows squabble in irksome rusty
cries. Blood smears the pavement. Rancid rot
belches the air. In the middle of
the street, a Possum, ironed out by
tires, sprawls its fleshy pink. Hyacinth
blooms crowd their beds in pastel curry,
periwinkle and coral clumps. They spray
the air with a teen boy's cheap cologne.
No breeze wipes the morning's smelly mix.

64
Tuesday, March 5, 2013

Sleep breaks into stone-fall clamor and
braces against dire dreams. Under cover of night's
cold shroud, predawn stealth prowls. A shadow's
on the move. It wobbles. It creeps. It
halts and seems to disappear. Wobbles
again. Again creeps. The back porch light
snaps on to search. Again the shadow
halts. The light sees two eyes briefly flash.
It sees silence—sees cold. It snaps off.
By contrast dawn's light is busy with
clues. Bricks on the compost lid strew the
ground. The lid is dumped. The ground grins corn
cobs, orange rinds, eggshells. *Here's a fine mess
to clean up*, it laughs. Dawn laughs right back.

65
Wednesday, March 6, 2013

crest and out into the city's wide
bare-limbed, crystal-cold air. The runner
races up the hill to crest into
a wide-faced embrace of ravishment,
sweat and glare. With its soundless trumpet
blast of frosted light, sun's advances
are abrupt and indiscriminate.
It flashes silver across roofs of
driveway cars. It glazes east-gazing
windows of every house in gleaming
frozen waterfalls. Its sheen splashes
the pavement slopes with alabaster
satin. Blindness is its other name.

66
Thursday, March 7, 2013

Noon's high south sun's drifting hawk-eye scans
everywhere. No camouflage of leaves
hides its search and strike. Green-brown nubs hint small
revolts. Their wee battalions hang from
tips of every twig. Sun's undone by
its own daily hubris. Its angle,
span, duration—all conspire a broad
green triumph.
              A Hawk dives its drone claws at
a Martin flock lifting a swirling black
halo above lines of bare Bradford
Pears. Helpless, the sun watches the hawk-swoop—
implacable crush of feathers and
bones—glide down to an old stump. Feeding
there, the Hawk stands in its own shadow.

67
Friday, March 8, 2013

Beneath green-tinged racks of antlers, tall
elms stand naked in late morning sun.
About their roots, new grass and tiny
rubies sprout. Wild Strawberries glint with
tangy juice and hard dirt-flavored seeds.
Ants scamper about the maze of bark.
Their sweetness is a different matter.
A Nuthatch struts headlong down the trunk
and stuffs his beak. Across the yard in
her soft earth nest, his mate pauses from
stuffing in dry grass. She calls her *yank
yank* song on its solitary parched
throat note. Tree bark drinks in the sun. It
pays no heed to berry, bird or bug.

68
Saturday, March 9, 2013

Haste's not in their vocabulary.
As the lagging flock dawdles through the
intersection, cars stall the noon rush.
With its red eye twirling, the police
car waits its turn too. Two geese halt in
their tracks then turn and dawdle back toward
the side they came from. With crystalline
polish across streets and yards, morning's
freshly showered air sits prim and crisp.
The geese strew their arrivals across
bright tender tufts. Thin sharp-edged bills tug
grass up. Like traffic, mid-morning moves
time's start and stop along. The geese make
themselves right at home and stay the day.

69
Sunday, March 10, 2013

Stretching its new found hour to its full
cloudless expanse, the evening light scores
long shadows across the barren back
yards that lie shoulder to shoulder in wait
for new grass imminences. Without
reason or rhyme, barren trees stagger.
Their shadows order their rhymes. As if
their dark straight elongations were the
reason sun chooses wistful reluctance,
their rhymes are regulated lines at
straight salutes. In its stream bank covert,
the gentle Dove pair softly croons a
nocturne to each other. The nocturne
lulls the shadows till the shadows fade.

70
Monday, March 11, 2013

New mown grass whistles barn loft through the
warming afternoon. With reunion
picnic cloth laid out, the back yard spreads
a wide chartreuse face of welcome. Guests
arrive. Across the shred of clipped grass,
a line dance of Robins bops. They plump
out raspberry vests and blouses. They
strut out spritely choreographies.
They dine. The spike of grass scent calls out
to the open shed door where the warm
mower parks: *Count them, I dare you. At
nineteen, their bobs and shifts force a
recount. Twenty maybe? Maybe just
sixteen. Who knows?* —Minutes don't stand still.

71
Tuesday, March 12, 2013

Checking off its clipboard assignments
of chores, late morning hovers over
shoulders everywhere. A Robin pair
beaks up tufts of dried out Pampas Grass
and wings them to the Japonica's
dark inner crotch. Another pair sorts
through the mound of fallen Cypress quills
and whisks them to the pine green Boxwood hedge.
Out back, the shorter pear tree strains to
push out wee small leaves. The side yard
plum sets out a few pink stars atop its
upper branches. In self-defense, it
flips back a glance across its shoulder
and explains, *Soon to come, more of same.*

72
Wednesday, March 13, 2013

Sky's Saharan dunes of nectarine
and periwinkle clouds billow and
sift from the eastern boundary of
light right up the arching dome. On the
theme of transience and present tense,
color and movement kaleidoscope
a graceful soliloquy. Its verbs mark
out the now that utterance marks out
as gone. Its colors are time's figments
made of light. Sky's bleaching out wins out
in the brevity of a drive time
short commute. The desert lightshow fades
into morning's full bloom meadows
of Cirrocumulus goose down white.

73
Thursday, March 14, 2013

The warming afternoon drinks up smells
of new mown roadside weeds and road-killed
rotting Possum flesh. It understands
how to hold judgment a close secret
because sundown is practicing to
dawdle and take its time. Afternoon
drinks the fermenting brew—with each sip,
more dazed. Its stupor spins furrows of
cut grass into straw and transforms blood
brown innards on the pavement into
black. It drifts along unresisting
currents of time that know no time, and
simply glad, it understands neither
how to sleep nor how to stay awake.

74
Friday, March 15, 2013

In generous swaths, dusk-lit strides move
between bare trees from the ample west.
They etch parallels of long slender
shadows across the infestations of
dead-nettles and wheat-straw grass. Tops of
barren trees beckon to the striding
light with unpretentious daubs of feeble
green. Like an oath fulfilled, light returns
their invitation with lime-juice splashes.
Rapacious in their disregard, two
squirrels swing on a high spindly oak
branch. They plunder pollen-ripe early
leaf-sprouts. Shreds of bright debris trickle
down through evening's luminous cool air.

75
Saturday, March 16, 2013

Siesta hour hums. Beneath the eave
hooks, the breeze sings lullabies to wind
chimes—both sets. The smaller set replies with
alto four-note riffs. The large five-foot
stainless rods intone Buddhist chants. The
breeze's words are of sun warmth, wafting
unperturbed from the broad clean sky, where
silent silver planes drift north and west.
A bright flash in the bare pecan tree
unveils a pair of eastern bluebirds.
Flicking wings of sky, the male lifts his
plum-white throat. His aria trills joy.
His mate sits unperturbed. Another
hour draws siesta's stretched hour out.

76
Sunday, March 17, 2013

The high noon hour's lazy warmth leads
clay-stained work shoes out the back gate. It
climbs through bud-tipped trees and brazen light
where woods give way to beat-down pads of
waist-high grass. Fresh deer prints press the mud.
Mats are thick and dry. Warmth dares to stretch
its back full length flat. Eyes take on sun's
full force. Polka dot cloud islands dot
the blueberry blue sky. Cool fingers
soak through the warmth. They creep seductions
up the spine from thighs to shoulder wings.
Syrupy wine scents of bog rot and
sweet straw implant their ether mask and
sink to porous borderlands of sleep.

77
Monday, March 18, 2013

Rain is sweater-cool and face-happy-
warm. It gathers fistfuls of street-light
light and strews them like moon sparks on the
ripples of a mountain lake. Across
the front yard, they light on peach and plum
blossoms. The trees glint in their candle
shrine and icon auras. Sun forgets
to rise but infuses the low clouds
with waxing shades from charcoal to slate
to herring-bone tweed. As day wakes to
half-light, the shimmering aura wanes.
Perfume pink replaces crystal glints
on the plum. Snowflake white, on the peach.
Rain wanes into drizzle. Day sets in.

78
Tuesday, March 19, 2013

Morning strolls out with a genteel smile
but weather fronts are fickle—north and
south. They switch and swipe like lawn tennis
rackets. Which will hold the court by day's
end? Anyone's guess. Mid-afternoon,
the wind swoops down from northern state line
counties, and with a couple well-aimed
sucker punches, decides the matter.
Decisively. A forecast for frost
menaces the predawn hours. Trays of
inch-high lettuce, tomatoes and
okras call to be brought in for the
night. Peach and plum blossoms say they'll take
their chances. Fragility's their strength.

79
Wednesday, March 20, 2013

Stoic and resolute, afternoon
will not release the chill morning wind
it clutched in its arms early in the
day. Held here, the wind can't go on with
plans to travel. The entente threatens
after midnight to settle in hard.
From rows of sprightly lettuce shoots, wee
voices call out for plastic caps to
huddle under. Meanwhile in bold plots
of reds, whites and purples, sentinel
tulips stand brave, defiant of pend-
ing terror. Afternoon inches down
one degree each hour. The flocks of
peach blossoms, in dread, hold their wee breaths.

80
Thursday, March 21, 2013

Beneath the piles of clouds and passing
showers, sunset strikes its iron hot and
the forge's coals glow. Dusk is wary
as its rabbit ears twitch like radars
unsure where danger lies. Nudging through
the wet grass, it nibbles whatever
of day still lingers. The sky rumbles.
An arrow flash darts from one dark cloud
to the next. Sunset shadows fidget.
They're etched now, now vanished, while above
the horizon's cooling embers, the
clouds spew the conflagration's thick smoke
in towering billows. They swirl
and climb until their black turns into night.

81
Friday, March 22, 2013

Smaller than midges that zigzag down
and up the air in colonies of
pin-point sparks, the business cards from Oaks
and Elms leave reminders they called. Their
pollen-sifting feather-light ash fills
sidewalk crevices and mortar cracks
of porch step bricks. Their ash silts up cars—
windows, roofs, hoods, trunk lids—all. It chums
with afternoon's face-warm air. They join
to weevil up nostrils. They creep in
sinus pouches. They pierce temples with
tight grips. Erupting from inside the
face's spasmodic inhaled gasp,
they explode in sneeze on sneeze on sneeze.

The Present Tense

82
Saturday, March 23, 2013

Sun's rapid shot across horizon's
bow drives off the frost and, aimed against
the crawl-space bricks of the south wall, sweats
the plastic sheets on hesitant trays
of inch-high lettuce, tomatoes and
okras. They wonder if this day will
shock their roots with garden soil and splats
of hard hose water. Patience waits its
reward. Despite drenching light's hint of
yes, forecasts sniff out jet stream's cold dip
no. They scorn the longings of this now's
now. Now's only now. With plastic off,
leaves bend into the light. The plastic
waits to hug them close from the chill dark.

83
Sunday, March 24, 2013

Those old house guests, chill and breeze, decide
to overstay. Their welcome's doubtful.
In lacy petticoats, the full bloom
line of Bradford Pears agrees to be
polite. As each stiff gust shivers down
the hill, their simpering curtsies say,
*Thank you kindly sire, it's a joy to
have you here.* The stage's high sky back-
drop cloudlessly smiles down. As its ears
are cocked for omens of imminent
departure, it reassures morning
that weather has its exits and its
entrances and in its time each plays
many parts. For the pears, cold comfort.

84
Monday, March 25, 2013

Between bare tops of wetland trees, Hawks'
swoops and glides cut arched paths. Their shadows
carve and slice the barren warmth-hungry
lawn's anticipation of the sun's
massage. The shadows' incisions leave
the blank grass helplessly intact. Late
afternoon sun's cold douse of stark light picks
over the last gauzy gasps of frail
daffodils. Their tissues are washed of
any color's name. Breezes bully
and slap them. They let go and fall. Lime
green leaf spikes outface the slaps. They stand
erect to nestle the colorless
blossom tatters of self-effacement.

85
Tuesday, March 26, 2013

The kitchen window imbibes coffee steam
rising from the gurgling pot. Streaked with
the black frieze of vertical trees, the
sky imbibes solid ice-hard air. The
dog dish is solid. Puddles on the
patio stones are solid. Beyond
the trees, horizontal cloud streaks glow.
Like ivory wax in thick long burning
candles, their opals are illusions.
They drift apart. Truth unveils. The wide
full-circle moon is their blazing cold
white wick. No flicker unsteadies its
large glow. No wind snuffs it. A second
coffee watches its descent. It's gone.

86
Wednesday, March 27, 2013

The moon in garish obesity
stares across the wide bleaching sky straight
into the torrid sun's outrageous
red surge. Dawn pirouettes on a stiff
toe in indecisive circles and
waits for a partner to step forward.
The moon rolls its orange rotundity
towards the western edge. As the sun's huge
blaze climbs higher, it melts toward whitish
yellow and sears eastbound eyes. Meanwhile
drivers headed west watch, right before
their eyes, tangerine transmogrify
into white. Day blushes, makes its choice
and floats to the sun's embrace: *I'm here.*

87
Thursday, March 28, 2013

Noon dries off the last lacy glitter
from morning's chilly shower. Its bold
bright warmth insists on cap and sunscreen.
Compliant and ruthless, the mower's
gas fumes shave swathes forth and back across
the new spunky grass. Cap and screen have
no defense against cloying spinnerets that
drape and clog the cool shadows beneath
old oaks. Mobs of dangling cankerworms
inch down necks warm under collar bands
and frolic in the sweat of hairy arms.
Their tiny wriggling feet dance to the
beat of voiceless singing: *This now is
ours. Noon has no purchase on our time.*

88
Friday, March 29, 2013

The sky blooms camellia cream from the
city's reflected electric glow.
Cloud blossoms jostle in balletic
puffs against the black drop of night. Their
choreographies gape apart in
sudden depths of space where, like conscience
pricks, stars, without blinking, transmit their
cacophonies of time. With curtains
jerked aside, the cold wind scratches its
icy claws on the hard glass. No lamp
is required to mark out a bathroom
path. Sleep chooses to wait up. All night
while stars scorn the now that windows watch,
creamy clouds dance across night's carpet.

89
Saturday, March 30, 2013

All morning, night's cold erects a blind
wall across the yard. Noon's mercury
tips up two more degrees. The sun's broad
cloudless swathes wash down through trees that have
postponed their greening up. The swathes are
powerless against the stubborn air.
Cold commands sun's touch, *Keep your distance.*
All at once, a silent summons breaks
the stalemate. Flitting in from every
side, thronging Chickadees and Robins
fly down. They jerk and bob around the
stubble grass. Exuberance of lunch
is their protest march. Glad to be of
some small use, sun keeps its still cold watch.

90
Sunday, March 31, 2013

All five sides of the dry chill-weary
backyard bare their chests to the bright and
useless morning sun. Birds are hard at
work—all five sides—plucking seeds—sprucing
nests—preening in the loose dirt. *Ready
or not,* they say, *here we are, back in
place.* Ordinariness stands firmly
in its place—all five sides. But then. Watch
now. Right along with the Chickadees,
Thrushes and Robins, a stranger—white
dollops on sleek black wings, orange-tawny
chest and glassy black head—settles in,
right at home. From where? How? A Grosbeak—
here—this here. A Grosbeak—now—this now!

April Journal

91
Monday, April 1, 2013

Sunrise reserves the middle of the
road for runners. Florid Bradford Pears
protect their rites of passage. Cascades
of front yard Azaleas hope their floes
of white will slip across the curb and
lap at weightless feet. The mid-pavement
rabbits crouch rigid with attention
as if assigned to greet them. As the
strides' last moment drives down, rabbits
dart off in quick shyness. Air is full of
twangling scents that brush perspiration
from the runners' eyes.
The Mourning Dove
laments lightly touch the inner pulse
of runner-ears. Content, the dove stays.

92
Tuesday, April 2, 2013

The open window hums dream-drowsy
song fragments to the dark soft rain. Rain's
dark response sings of lighter blankets.
Its tiny feet on the deck table
tap out tireless delicate polkas
and methodical polonaises.
Lost in the gloom of tree trunks and low
stationary clouds, a Possum's clicks float
in—desolate and muffed—on the sweet
aromatic damp. Farther out in the
woods, cluck-cluck cluckings reply. The
conversation is a slow tennis
volley's dream-drowsy antiphony.
First light wakes birdsong window freshness.

93
Wednesday, April 3, 2013

Noon sun floats sweet breaths into the porch
swing shade. The tumbler of unsweet tea
streaks its sides with ice sweat. Breezes lisp
questions to the wind chimes. They ping and
pong enigmatic Zen replies. Eyes
adrift in enigmas of their own
hear, but do not listen. Sweat puddles
around the tumbler's base on the dry
deck floor. From the awning roof, lacey
leaf shreds sprinkle silt on the breeze. It's
started. There. Again this year. Like a
boy's crammed pockets, with its sloppy loose
fragility, the half constructed
Wren nest is stuffed in its hidden fold.

94
Thursday, April 4, 2013

Methodically all day, rain washes
slow spaghetti streams of chill red-clay
down bare patches in the slopes of lawns.
It waxes the soft gray wing sheen of
feeding Doves. It scruffs up the fur of
scrawny squirrels clawing up mud holes
for old nuts. As school busses take turns
blocking the intersection, children
jump down the steps and dart like matted
kittens between driveway cars to the
shelter of porches—shivering and
shirking. The now of change holds fixed its
lens with each refocused change. Presence
is as transient as permanence.

95
Friday, April 5, 2013

Along the sun washed street, commuters
greet the parade of late afternoon's
replicated houses. They approach
and uniformed Bradford Pears stand guard
like stately sentinels in full dress
whites. They salute as each car drives past.
Crew cut lawns replicate their stately
silhouettes.
Sun despairs of rigid
conformities. It prefers to light
dark crannies, hide mildewed corners and
sprawl cacophonies of shadows from
gangly half-dead oaks.
Up across the
grassy berm's wild Phlox's blue carpet,
from the other side, blue spills ripple.

96
Saturday, April 6, 2013

Late afternoon's warm breeze rocks upper
branches of the window-high bush. They
scratch fingernails on the bedroom glass.
Below the sill, in the three prong crotch,
perches a grass-fleeced cup. It sways. Out
of the blue, while the window's back is
turned, three blue eggs appear. The sinking
sun pokes fingers through the shadows. It
watches. Its touch is patient. Its warmth
waits. As shadows drop, a flutter hops
down. It settles in—dun breast—folded
Robin wings. Out of the side of her
motionless head, a glass black bead keeps
peeled on the window above her head.

97
Sunday, April 7, 2013

As if it thought the clearing in the
woods across the stream bridge were a pond,
sky tosses down its narcissism
as blue as Catalina blue. Through
the cloudless space, sky and clearing face
off. Sunlight's the gawking referee.
En masse Deadnettles' rampant tiny
blooms overflow damp clay with smelts-packed
shimmering so dense the clearing ripples.
The joke's on the sun. His vanity
has no pool to spill his face in. The
clearing is for strolling shoes. Their soft
pressure sweeps piney mint aromas
up through damp cool air. Air drinks its fill.

98
Monday, April 8, 2013

The massage of noon sun kneads
fingers deep into in the stooping gardener's back.
As its warmed blanket of dried leaves is
raked from the wintered compost, sweet-and-
sour steam floats up. Sun laps the steam. Steam
laps the stooping nostrils. A loose coil
of dark naked compost shifts, uncoils,
twitches three feet of gleaming black skin
and shoos its Rat-Snake-self back down the
hole into the warm inner sanctum
of the compost pile. The stooping rake
takes one deep long breath then sweeps off the
rest of the leaf cover. Pitchfork scoops
fill the wheelbarrow with black pungent steam.

99
Tuesday, April 9, 2013

Troweled furrows in the damp bed of mixed
compost and soil open rows to seeds
spaced inch by inch with the precision
of bare finger pinches. Fingers fold
fresh compost over the slender gash.
They thump. Damp knees waddle slowly to
the row end. In the moist soft cool, they
ache. In the sun's massage, the bent back
luxuriates. The fence post holds a
firm shoulder as the aches stand up, lean
and stretch the spine out. The hose nozzle
holds a steady fine spray. In return
the bed holds up its pungent dark face
and rainbows of stained glass mist soak in.

100
Wednesday, April 10, 2013

The indecisive breeze tugs at a
few peach blossoms but quickly lets go.
Bemused it watches school buses pass.
Cars scurry late to jobs. It waits for
them to get to where they need. Now and
then it coughs and sputters. Suddenly
it grasps hold of its conductor wand
and Azaleas fling up their Moulin Rouge
skirts and petticoats. Milkshake pink churns
and sloshes. Magenta simmers in
the green leaves. Scarlet brazenly flirts.
White strives to be flurries. The wand thumps
the air and tries to ignore it's a
mere breeze. The dancing chorus is thrilled.

101
Thursday, April 11, 2013

Warm evening spreads soft flannel mittens of
steady rain across the darkening
walks and lawns and busy flowerbeds.
As if weighed by sadness, the common
Peonies lay down taffy pink faces
in the mud. Their brazen Chinese cousins
spread variegated crepe petals to
stand wide and tall and drink their fill. On
the porch rail, tea rose vines glint with small
red sparks. Discussing forecasts for the
night, their plentitude chatters forth and
back: *sterner peltings*; or, *soft fadings
into dark fog*; or, *ambushes of
lightening to rupture sky and slap trees*.

102
Friday, April 12, 2013

Viburnum fans the evening above
the stream that whips cream froth around the
rock bend only to run on in slow
clarity. Breezes breathe after-swills
of Riesling's apple sweetness, and then
like petals of invisible dew,
they cast them off with grand abandon.
The blossoms forming tight nosegays, like
swirls of soft ice cream, hang along the
higher branches, where a pair of Blue
Jays sits creaking quiet rusted pump
handles to each other. In the branch
crotch beneath them, a half built cup-bowl
nest awaits morning's summons to chores.

103
Saturday, April 13, 2013

Behind the vacant for-lease house, tree-
tops regale themselves in amethyst
wigs. High above blank windows, splendid
sunlit Wisteria waterfalls
ripple light from the bleached noon sky. The
windows gawk at fluff balls of white
Dandelions and shaggy grass. On
the driveway dirt, sprawled in a furry
gray puddle, a dead cat excites the
haggle of two gleaming crows. They shove
elbows at each other and tear out
intestine shreds. A second tawny
cat peeps from the broken crawl space door.
The lavender spill keeps flowing down.

104
Sunday, April 14, 2013

Morning's hints of mist invite jackets.
Through small greening of trees whose leaves are
more than promises and less than facts,
they slink about in silver. The wide gate
gulps from the jug of early light and
blossoming trees. On the gate post, the
abandoned mug exhales coffee steam.
Like dance contestants stepping to the
crowded floor, in splashy magenta
party shirts, Redbuds dot the woods. They
reach out hands to Dogwood partners in
starch-white ruffled gowns with small brown stains
that won't wash out. Tensed and ready, they
wait the up-beat. Stranded coffee cools.

105
Monday, April 15, 2013

Dawn's glow unfurls its quiet in a
fuchsia gown, its ears as keen as spice
aromas. There, where the underbrush
along the stream is cleared and trees are
teased with chartreuse blush, five lean high-flanked
does and two white puffy tailed fawns
munch clumps of grass. They're held in auras
and solemnities and silence, while
suspended in this now, the upper
window anticipates their skitter
into vanishing distances of
fleetness and light at a car door's slam
or school bus's brakes. The window aches
for stillness to freeze dawn in a frame.

106
Tuesday, April 16, 2013

Next to the posthole scars of the fresh
vinyl fence, sunlight pricks out dollops
of needlepoint color. Folding their
spidery leaves beneath their chins, young
Dandelions nestle lemon tart
puffs close to the warm soil. Violets
peek out beneath dark green funnel-cups.
Wild Strawberries dangle on wiry
threads. Atop spindly stems, liquid drops
of sun spill glints of wax on outstretched
Buttercups. The fence slaps noon glare straight
at the porch swing's squint. Dropped from the tight
nest in its canopy fold, Wren poop
on the canvas glowers white right back.

107
Wednesday, April 17, 2013

Morning's chilly haze steps into sun,
makes a brief elegant curtsy with
shy smile and shy eyes, and rushes from
the sky. Afternoon climbs up
with bounding clouds. Its plot thickens. The
mob grows agitated. Its tension
wants riot. As birds hush and skitter
into low bushes, the dark grumbling
gets louder. When the sky spills its guts,
no canon salutes, no camera flares.
The surprise attack cascades the school
bus glass and overwhelms whipping blades.
The bus brakes mid-street. Dim red warning
beams blink out into unseen blindness.

108
Thursday, April 18, 2013

Along the outside wall, the window
calls to the deck swing: *look to the breeze—
there. It is tugging at the loose locks
of your canopy.* Content with small
realignments, the breeze shakes out its
gentle trajectories. It nips at
the Azalea's carmine petals. It
tears them loose to flutter in gimpy
brief flights. Like cherry juice they trickle
into crevices of walkway stones.
Tender white Dogwoods tremble on cue.
To acknowledge, with a Wren nest in
its hair, the window's call, the swing smiles
back as if to say: *I see. I know.*

109
Friday, April 19, 2013

From hem to cap, the trees are dressed at last. ever
They wear styles current for the season.
Their greens defy good lexicons. The
late morning sun takes its sweet time to
wedge open a gap through their crowded
lavish frocks. It showers light across
the sparks of pear blossoms that dangle
precariously from the meshed twigs.
Suddenly with the impertinence
of a sneeze, their white confetti floats.
With neither plan nor system, they cut
their ties and let go. For the rest of
the day, the barren dirt spreads itself
with a tablecloth of frothy lace.

110
Saturday, April 20, 2013

The glass black bead keeps peeled on the late
morning's window above her head with its
blinds slid wide. With her chest feathers fluffed,
she climbs to the nest brim. An upper
branch jerks and her mate hops down. His beak
aims its long tweezers at two wide bright
orange spread-scissor gawks. Behind all the
straining eagerness a plump blue pearl
protrudes—sealed and blind. Like the morning's
drifting cloud puffs, the ordinariness
reconfigures itself moment by
moment in the presence of the ever-
present present. Its sole task is to
busy itself with mere astonishment.

111
Sunday, April 21, 2013

Doing its work in silent stealth, dew sneaks
in even before horizon's watch-
tower starts to spy out evidence
of sunrise. When the slippered walk down
to the curbside shrubs, coffee mug in
hand, fetches back the damp ink-smudged news
from yesterday, teardrop pearls lie
in the laps of the Smoketree's sprouts of
grayish-purple leaves. Scarlet, glazed with
crystallized sugar, can't hold back the
Azalea gush from top to toe. *See,*
it shouts, *I am here.* The sole news that
memory's yesterday carries back
with it is smudged—not quite fit to read.

112
Monday, April 22, 2013

With gentle coaxing strokes, afternoon's
breeze brushes the panting puppy-faced
irises with their three tongues hanging
out. Carpenter Bees in yellow and
black jackets are elated at their
extravagance of color. They hang
stationary buzzing bubbles mid-
air and then dive down blossom's furry
yellow throats. They pick and choose along
the staggered rows of tissue faces:
indigo streaked with white, punch pink, egg
yolk yellow, tangerine. As breeze stiffens
their carnival stage, they jostle stick
puppet faces with wide panting tongues.

113
Tuesday, April 23, 2013

Rain strides in vertical formations
straighter than the afternoon trees
it elbows past. It marches down streets
and parades across yards. With a snare drum's
riffing tattoo, its persistent boot
treads click heels on deck floors and porch roofs.
Beneath its eave, the door throws open
arms to grab the pelting warmth. It breathes
in damp hay scent of yesterday's mown
grass. It burns with desire to submit,
to throw its insatiable face up,
to run drenched and barefoot so fast its
mouth overflows like a spigot—to
swallow gulp after gulp after gulp.

114
Wednesday, April 24, 2013

The dawn sun scatters arabesques of
splotchy brightness across the pavement
and fresh lawns. For the time being the
air is too busy to heed the light.
It tosses cheeps, chuffs and ricochets
of wind chime bird chortles from cedars
to hollies and back. The tree tops glow
in Wisteria's lavender haze
above the high wire pair of Doves
who turn synchronous necks in precise
slow calligraphies, and precisely
turn by turn, coo their satin-soft coos.
Ears are busy with the commotion
in the air. Sunlight busies the earth.

115
Thursday, April 25, 2013

Beyond the backyard gate, canopies
of woodland trees lift fresh swaying crowns,
black and lofty, against the darkly
lavender cream sky. Along the tops,
over gently sloshing waves, the white
wholeness of the moon slowly rolls its
florescent ball. The sweater clutches
its reluctant buttons tightly to
its chest. It strives to fend off the night's
settling chill. It strives to lengthen out
the unsung orotund presence of
its presence here. It fails. Chill drives it
back indoors. With no haste in sight, moon's
dispassion turns its back and rolls on.

116
Friday, April 26, 2013

Like snuggly soft shadows, night casts its
potpourri of nameless perfumes in
small gulps of breeze through the screen of the
slid back balcony doors. Stewy steam
seeps faintly in on rosemary whiffs.
Drafts of Hyacinth honey bully
their way right through. Viburnum's dusky
warble flickers along for the ride.
With each flutter's generosity,
like memories too faint to locate
in any specificity of
time, the wind chimes' four well-harmonized
tenors shuffle through their repertoire
of unpremeditated changes.

117
Saturday, April 27, 2013

Lying prone and facing up, the mid-
morning backyard hammock watches the
gem complete its setting and fully
regale itself with light. The sapphire's
breathless blue in classic cushion shape
beams down. It glints like sun on rippling
mountain lakes. A dozen emerald prongs
cut the elegance in marquis tips
to hold the sky in place. Held in leaf-
drenched stillness they too gleam. Encircled
in its setting's rest of lights,
the stillness fills air—and hour. Facets
bejewel the upturned face while beneath
drowsy lids, the rocking hammock naps.

118
Sunday, April 28, 2013

With no desire for haste, night grubs at
rotting logs along the vines that snare
the creek with its clay-brown midnight rush
of cloudburst run-off. Night snuffs around
and, time to time, its waif Possum-call
clucks faintly across the wet woods floor.
The elsewhere of night's loneliness, time
to time, barks faintly back. High in the
gray light, bats jolt and jerk. Trees are half
awake with young dark leaves. Nursing in
burrows and matted deer fawn thickets,
night is half asleep. The only haste
present here, gargling and sloshing
to itself, is the creek's frantic churn.

119
Monday, April 29, 2013

A contest of height and white blocks the
downhill view of the creek. They compete
for attention. The foot high
snowball Hydrangea cascades its white
so thick branches sag. Overflows of
cotton soccer balls freeze their downward
plunge and do not plunge. Beside it, just
as tall, the Japanese Viburnum
layers its shelves of white against shelves
of fresh lime leaves. Shoulder to shoulder
they grab the burst of sunrise sun and
glow. Work-bound cars halt to gawk. They *aah*
and *ooh*. The trees nudge each other and
whisper, *Just see what we've gone and done.*

120
Tuesday, April 30, 2013

Rain's slow inevitability
sounds nothing so much as steady rain.
The way damp kitchens greet the gargle
of drawn-out pots of steaming stew, the
sun porch roof welcomes rain's entropic
lullaby. Windows welcome the scrim
of rain-gauze as it wipes out pollen
from wee pockets in the air. Pristine
green pecan blossoms gleam in their sprigs
of tiny emerald periwigs. Fig
trees' slender branches glint with pristine
emerald nubs. This side of consciousness,
—just—time's slide digs in for a day of
high pitched greens and low pitched lullabies.

May Journal

121
Wednesday, May 1, 2013

Without pause to catch a breath, rain is
the ever-present daylong present
tense. Vertical shafts immerse the air.
From time to time, clouds rumble up, crack
and flare. From time to time, hypnotic
chopsticks patter faint bamboo taps. It
has no drive. Steadiness is a
calming voice. It saturates. It floods.
melting lawn into the stream's sloshing
brown overflow, it swells a shallow
pond's embrace. No shift of light or sun
disturbs its timelessness. Miasma
is its name; persistent gentle warmth,
its unbearably lulling caress.

122
Thursday, May 2, 2013

All along the bank, dawn silently
steps through the foggy dark to leave its
tell-tale tracks. Day wakes late with mud in
its yawning mouth. Its torrential dreams
bequeath hung-over dark residues
beneath its eyes. As cheerful as a
mascara-eyed waitress with mugs of
tangy coffee steam, the stream over-
flows with chatter. Its mocha cream is
chock full of leaves and twigs. At the bend,
it churns up chocolate batter. Cut deep
in the bank-side mud are cloven prints
for toes, and dew-claw holes for heels. Each,
with its small tan puddle, tells a tale.

123
Friday, May 3, 2013

Air is hung-over from its debauch
of rain. Its cold perspiration
lies in its own exhaustion. Longing
to greet sunset's setting show, the late
afternoon window watches orange brown
sky turn orange. Beneath the sill, the pair
of fledgling Robins spreads dappled wings.
Alone and thwarted, they shove. As if
a boat tipped on a wave, one bird tips
from the rim and falls. Its feathers
tumble through the bush. Shoving itself
overboard, the second bird dives. Beneath
the window's eye, wet grass pillows them.
Above it, sky's western lid blurts flames.

124
Saturday, May 4, 2013

Rain thickened grass stretches up
dashing Harlequin green arms. Clouds pack up
and drive east. Sun spatters the wide yard
with motley paint ball smears of emerald.
Swollen damp, the grass is in no haste to
dry out. Its engorged dirt holds close the
slippery pantaloons. The mower
huffs up the slope. It struggles through the
profusion of rain-warmed growth. Blades choke
up. Engine chokes out. Mulch and juice choke
the machine's gaped throat. Across and back,
it stalls. Starter cord jerks it back to
life. The morning's meadow is conquered.
Tamed, the lawn shows off its best manners.

125
Sunday, May 5, 2013

Crinkling, drying thin and heading to
their land of the forgotten, blooming
Wisterias scattered through the trees
watch their better days sift away. They
are neither yesterday nor never.
In crass contempt of them, morning breaks
into now's arpeggiated fife,
piccolo and flute trills. The wide yard,
Cypresses on one side, Apples the
other, hosts quadraphonic Robin
choirs. Their responses and calls sing out
hello and sunrise. Full of song, the
lofts have no time yet for the ant and
worm breakfast spread across lawn's buffet.

126
Monday, May 6, 2013

Like kindling taking life inside a
sky-high funeral pyre, sun burrows
its lapping tongues of flame through the stacks
of dark brown clouds. Night's all-night drunken
carouse hangs heavy in Viburnum and
Hydrangea trees. Their branches drag
bedraggled skirts. They slosh the ground. The
toddling okra shoots float frail mud-clogged
leaves. With tan, pink and blue broken heads,
irises lie ignominious
in the soggy grass. Voiceless matins
chant monodies, and from libation
sensors, green aromas steam up in
the vapors of washed-silk's clearing air.

127
Tuesday, May 7, 2013

The mower trudges through tall rain engorged
weeds and grass. It skids on early morning's
slopes like grease spilled floors. The blades gag on
the thick wet concoction. Savory hay spews
barn loft furrows out. Well-worked
shoes soak green stains up into squishy
socks and blistering toes. Merciless,
the steaming engine grinds and trudges
on. Helplessness sprawls before its path.
Three-foot tall pink and blue Irises
lie broken in the lawn. The mower
gulps them down. Bright confetti shreds cough
out and stick to damp sweatpants legs. All
morning, morning is a stopped stop watch.

128
Wednesday, May 8, 2013

Coaxing lawn chairs to stretch their legs and
hammocks to sway in half-asleep shut
eyes, sun lays out sheets of warmth across
the backyard. Evening procrastinates
about stretching out shadows. By the
fence, the wheelbarrow's collected rain
squiggles with mosquito larvae.
A pair of rabbits' caution stops and
starts up the slope. They find the clover
patch by the heat pump. They munch sweetness.
Throwing caution aside, the smaller
rabbit scampers to the Boxwood's shade.
The game is on. She hides. The larger
chases. He finds. Breeding ends the day.

129
Thursday, May 9, 2013

Midmorning comes trotting down into
the backyard but no invitation
is required and brunch is very near
ready, just waiting for scones to warm.
Shadows from the predawn downpour still
clutch coolness to their chests with mittens
of March. But it is May. It is the
birthday of tomorrow's yesterday
and of the clock hands' meltdown. It spreads
its wide mottled skirts. Spanked down by the rain,
the young tomato leaves have lifted
and the tiny yellow stars beneath
are squinting. The scones are warm. Taste one.
Grass is steaming faintly in the sun.

130
Friday, May 10, 2013

Across the sky, dulcet white fleece
spreads out light evenly from edge to
edge. Its sheet is veil enough to hide
the bevies of noon shadows that wish
to slink along the sides of hedges and
beneath tree domes whose breezes play like cats.
They yearn for shadows' play and keep their
whispers to themselves. Liking shade and
sun alike, impartial Carpenter
Bees delve burrows in the railings. Wee
sawdust mounds pile the deck floor. With no
shadows to reflect their forlorn *pas de
deux,* bee pirouettes hang solos in
the air. Treetops wave silent applause.

The Present Tense

131
Saturday, May 11, 2013

The sparse grass pad of dirt sips just the right
amount of warmth. When the moment's ripe,
it coughs up low flying Miner Bees
from sieve-like pencil holes. They are old
friends come back to visit, so ropes of
gold Lady Banks' roses call to their
gold tufted manes: *come cuddle with us
and drift on our waves of afternoon
stupor.* Sunlight sprinkles swirls of gold
midges in mist sprays above their heads.
It looks deeply through the greening trees
to the west horizon and decides
for now in the goodness of good time
their rendezvous must wait awhile—still.

132
Sunday, May 12, 2013

Light from porches meanders from yard
to back yard between linked-arm burly-
shouldered shadows. Fences cower. Like
cousins at a party, the shadows
fuss and gossip. Their silent laughter
is time-honored sport. Surreptitious
coolness infiltrates to crash the fun.
But can't. In newly donned velvet robes
above the darkness of trees, breezes
tussle the high coiffures against the
jostle of night-lit cloud mounds. Stars click
pin points on. Then vanish. A bitten
lip of bitter moon glows slender
white above horizon's blackened west.

133
Monday, May 13, 2013

As morning's high tide rises, shadows
slink beneath full-coiffed trees. Resonant
arpeggios lift and fall across
the neighborhood in busy geese flights.
Their discontent cracks and barks across
high stratus wisps and blue, forth and back,
from pond to pond. The street end trucks are
suited up and call their geese echoes
at the gate to release them from the
depot yard for a day's good workout.
Sun's wake-up call stuns the branch-pile and
lifts its privy gate. Glad to oblige,
the Kingsnake's onyx and brass gleam slips
out to shop the frog holes for its lunch.

134
Tuesday, May 14, 2013

The deck chair on the shaded upper
porch lies gentle in its aches. The hung-
over breath of hay hangs gentle on
its heavy lids and drifting eyes. It
recalls morning's dredge through the rain-high
grass as the mower sputtered and coughed up
furrows. Mown rows stretch from yard end to
yard end and the tree encircled maze
in between. They're the riff-raff of the
morning's noisy hours. Submerged beneath
the rudderless hawk-skiff as it sails
its currents of stillness, just this side
of sleep, afternoon's slow aromas
holds vigil with memory's small trace.

135
Wednesday, May 15, 2013

Water stiffens the hose's spine, chokes,
then sputters the nozzle. Sun lifts its
lid of light across the roof. Shadows
creep backwards behind the walls. Like a
shimmering gothic arch, water settles
into parabolic streams. With wrist
turn—and body lean—beams of water
flow down across tomato towers,
okras and beds of early herbs. A breeze
fondles arm and leg hairs with silver
mist. Grass's thick pelt grows spongy. With
one firm kick—each foot—thongs fly off. The
nozzle sprays ice water on legs and
feet. Toes wade and giggle in the grass.

136
Thursday, May 16, 2013

Grass drags dark green shadows to the creek's
crumbling bank. The narrow stream flows dark
green gulps and mumbles. On the other
side, blackness carves out deep coverts
beneath leaning trees and snag toothed vines.
In the gloaming, the pre-dawn moonshine
daubs in white roses. Their erratic
creamy pale clusters overhang
the creek. Like silent soft purring, their
sweet aroma slips through porous night
damp. Tucked on a high nest, the mournful
purr of Doves croons covert gray replies.
As if no farewell were to arrive,
darkness stands its ground this side of dawn.

137
Friday, May 17, 2013

Conspiring together, street lights, porch
lights, school bus lights—through ginger tang of
air and its cool smile—flit and fleck the
heavy dew in giggling randomness.
The clover patch in the lawn holds a
spark at the crotch of each three leaves. The
miniature rose trellis spills glitter
down its long apron front to the ground.
Parked fresh from yesterday's car wash, the
dark roof shows off its sequined robe of
glass-clear pearls. In the band of gray light
atop the dark blur of trees, bats take
lingering dives before retiring
to their perches for a good day's rest.

138
Saturday, May 18, 2013

Old colleague—stalker—pal—the heat climbs
down to the yard. It says how glad it
is to be back. It grabs gulps of sun
and splats them down to wilt tomato
towers and pungent beds of herbs. Okras
limp in shame. Heat knows its way around
the yard and remembers where to scorch
the grass and how to press hot irons on
granite stepping stones. Its first bully
day back on the job's a farce. Humid
air swells its lungs. Haze swells its clouds—clouds,
their cloudburst. The brief shower turns
to face evening with slaps of cool shade.
Okra resurrections stand up straight.

139
Sunday, May 19, 2013

The late afternoon wind is scratchy
like the trimmed hollies box-cropped
in their rigid barriers between
two lawns. Their leaf-spikes warn, *Run your bare
arm against me at your peril.* Wind's
warning is about cold fronts pushing
in and thermometers dropping and
sweaters. The sky sweeps away slips
of slender clouds. The compass points, and
points between, pull a seamless blue
sheet down around each tight horizon.
Across tree tops cell phone towers crackle
silent scarlet lights. The hedge's last
few berries, too, whisper small scarlets.

140
Monday, May 20, 2013

On tomato urns in the yard, dawn
showers are no longer memories.
Lunchtime errands hardly disturb the
quiet street. Sun's downcast glare is as
harmless as the small jingling of wind
chimes. A Chipmunk darts about the grass.
Untouched sandwich and steaming tea catch
the peripheral corner of their
hungry eye. The chaise longue sits up and
turns its head. Like a crisp slice of lime,
gleaming, an Anole glides along
the fence's white cross beam. Full-faced with
sun, it halts and croons its neck. The slim
tongue flickers out and in. Lunch starts now.

141
Tuesday, May 21, 2013

Greens are darkly liquid in their rills
and drooping night-rain shades. Their drenched and
heavy tops just manage to hold up
the soggy weight of morning clouds. They
are a roof on verge of collapse. Soaked
into the bloated folds, sunrise is
swallowed. Air holds more water than it
can. From her brief business, the dog comes
in spraying mist from her fusty fur.
With gaps of neither gray nor blue, the
closed ring of linked arms and bowed shoulders
surrounds the house with greens. Every pull-
draped window looks out to the protective
encirclement of contralto jades.

142
Wednesday, May 22, 2013

Mid-afternoon decides to up and
play the bully. It takes its bat and
cracks a thunder ball across the lost
horizon. Called foul, its second try
goes down in a half-hearted grumble.
No home run. It rolls up a cloud as
dark as compost and lets it loose to
lumber about on elephantine
legs. It gives up and wanders off. With
not a drop to show for it, the
whole act is a cardboard charade. The
silenced birds come out again and trill
and thrill from every side as the sun's
cascade of spotlight light courses down.

143
Thursday, May 23, 2013

With the sky just standing there decked out
in its best dress blues and jotting down
meticulous notes, the trees and wind
take control of the afternoon. The
leaves dance a manic ragtime shimmy.
From bouffant crowns to flowing veils and
skirts, their sequins scintillate like chips
of emerald glass. As the cold front strides
across the Piedmont, air empties out its
dust, humidity and pollen. Like
companions in conversation, half-
unspeaking half-speaking, it fixes its
attention onto listening and
it breathes clarity of spring water.

144
Friday, May 24, 2013

Evening dreams itself in a child's brain.
All its memorials are now. Sweet
barbeque and charcoal smoke echo
across the backyards as *plop, plop, swoosh*
basketballs float through driveway hoops. Small
dogs yip up at bouncing trampolines.
Laughter shrills to the early weekend
countdown toward year's first big divide. The
child brain dreams night never comes. Sun lies
low across the sky and never sets.
Tiredness never wears him down. As
the large dog's slow lope to her water
bowl lays down her head on outstretched paws,
the child is called in to bath and bed.

145
Saturday, May 25, 2013

Fog draws blinds down across the street and
all its lawns. It cancels sunset and
with every star, flips off the switch. Back
porch lights huddle in feeble cotton
balls of glow. Near the broad leafed stand of
figs, the yard light forgets where it is
and what it sees. The grape vine stretches
gropingly on its inauspicious
trellis. The sounds of cars slink past as
if shame were hiding under their dark
hoods. Backed up to the porch door, the cat's
tail slowly lashes the black screen.
Against invisibility and
nippy damp, her wan complaint persists.

146
Sunday, May 26, 2013

Night strides deep through silences until
a helicopter's purring becomes
obsessive roar. Its hawk arcs roam the
open sky above expressway ramps
a half-mile distance. Like a thick white tongue
licking thick cream, its beam burrows through
mounds of fog. It seeks the dark roadside
trauma and makes porch lights snap on and
doors stand open wide. Like ocean froth
washing the knees of boulders, fog flows
between dim trees. It inundates parked
cars and lawns. Above it, with the thrill
of sirens on the prowl, blackness streams
up through space to lap at clear high stars.

147
Monday, May 27, 2013

Sun broadcasts across splotchy thick fog
with snow-blinding ferocity. It
conspires eagerly in fog's under-
cover plots. Familiar road bends lure
passing cars to abrupt honking halts.
Penned-up dogs volley their moon-howls in
reply. House roofs brush locks of thinning
silver hair. Loose strands float off. They snare
low branches. Lying in wait to trip
tires and throw steering wheels off course, they
sink into the mud of the roadside
ditch. With roof lights snapping yellow out
of nowhere, the first school bus of the
day emerges from the light's white wall.

148
Tuesday, May 28, 2013

The back gate winks flirtations to the
woods. Too busy to flirt back, they shake
their windblown heads. The gate swings wide and says,
I'll come out anyway. The path trips
up through fallen rotting limbs. The stand
of pines chatters its constant chatter:
whoosh—whoosh. The path loses its last trace
where the creek greets trodden marsh grass:
glug—glug. As sunset opens its bag
of stains and pigments, the stumpy dead
trees in the marsh swoop up flurries of
rasps and caws. Above their nest, Hawks rise
and sink with news of a full day. The
path stays busy in its present tense.

149
Wednesday, May 29, 2013

The morning's orgasmic tease begins with
delicious whiffs of sweat. After a
second coffee it starts early with
forehead beads and kneeling to dig
intransigent weeds around the knee-
high okras. Trickles beneath the cap
along the nape run in synchrony
with turning compost in the bin. Its
insistence grows. Hauling and stacking
fallen branches in the far back lawn and
drenching the t-shirt chest relish their
shared hour. After pulling vines from shrubs,
wet heat and eagerness glow as they
embrace the rushing hose's cold gasp.

150
Thursday, May 30, 2013

Like noon facing back at the morning's
last shadows and forward toward the sun's
high tide, the pair of Doves sits on the
power line above the Cypress trees—
each beside the other. One faces
out to the woods across the street and
coos. The other, back turned, looks inward
to survey the lawn and roof as if
the vista were its cool reply each
turn at cooing that it takes. Their soft
gray dialogue, mannerly and calm,
turns one way; the sun's searing white burns
an opposing trail. The window
thermometer throbs its upward climb.

151
Friday, May 31, 2013

Late morning breezes riff the vines and
branches playing hide and seek with small
promises tucked beneath wide open
leaves. Beside weathered fence slats, yellow
winks along cucumbers and squash vines that
trail down from well-composted mounds. Their
open sweetness imbibes the bees' probes
and kisses. Pale green and pencil thin,
pears dangle beneath perky leaves set
to start long itineraries toward
ripeness. Fig nubs stand, beneath dark green
umbrellas, erect and hard. Neither
rhyming nor reasoning, breezes riff
streaks of movement down and up each tree.

June Journal

152
Saturday, June 1, 2013

Across the creek, sunrise sprinkles crisp
light through the jingling canopy of
leaves. With hooves too big for their ankles,
two kittenish fawns trail beside
their mothers' sides. Their oversized ears
are so close that one swift twitch grazes
a maternal flank. Each swatch of grass
looks up. It munches. It twists its neck.
It stares with black marble glass eyes. Each
cautious step is shadow dappled and
sun struck. When the second floor window
taps, their tawny frames do not bolt. They
drift off, like forgetfulness, into
the brush. Behind them shadows close in.

153
Sunday, June 2, 2013

Night's shrinking band of sky sets up shop
between the tree-lined horizon and
the tent-top shelf of clouds. The oblique
triangle of Venus, Jupiter
and speck-white Mercury drift behind
the northwest mound of trees. Applause
ends. The sky's silence steps forward in
black. Behind the cloud tarp, the sequin
gown of stars hides. Binoculars sit
abandoned on the deck table. The
show is over. The bedroom door slides
and snaps its lock. Clouds ooze farther down
across the slice of sky and slowly
inundate what's left of memory.

The Present Tense

154
Monday, June 3, 2013

Aloft in the old oak, a dead branch
catapulted sometime overnight
and wedged into the fig tree's spider sprawl
of arms. Suddenly out of the noon's
silence, like a dad's abrupt call to
a child in a field of sea-blue corn-
flowers, the branch's hull cracks, the prow
lurches forward—sinks—stalls lower down.
The fig's electric will shivers. Its
small green bells clink in gleeful silence.
A second iceberg jolt rocks the hull. Hear
the thud! The branch jerks down, splits apart
and hits the bare dirt spot by the tree
like the last sentence of a story.

155
Tuesday, June 4, 2013

The arthritic old oaks swashbuckle
and slash septuagenarian arms.
Their sharp croaks call up to the winds and
clouds invoking rites of late after-
noon downbursts. They whip their leaves downside
up and shush the birds into covert
crannies and silent nooks. Like useless
rotting memories, dead limbs crack and
fall down in flagellating chunks on
top of the fig tree's turmoil of leaves.
Like shingles, torn bark strews the grass with
ants' frenzied disorientations.
With wads of angry spit, the first rain
splats hit. Sky's pail tips. Sky's bucket pours.

156
Wednesday, June 5, 2013

Humping along in tandem sleek black pairs,
six Starlings glean the fresh mown lawn. They
harvest ants and seeds. Dusk-lit grass glows
in jade shadows. Onyx feathers gleam.
Bobbing beaks flash yellow stabs and pricks
like toy machines. In a parallel
with the Starlings' now, with different laws
another now presides. Ankle-high
moist tang of hay teems with conclaves of
mosquitoes gathering to ply their
trade in thirst and blood. They too know how
best to stab and prick. Their now hungers
too. Each shape of now is as supple
as who observes—what stands where—and why.

157
Thursday, June 6, 2013

The sun creeps its sloth claws down through trees
and offers to shadows lounging out
beyond the porch, sound advice on how to
arrange themselves. A wine-gray purple
licks up the forest green of the block
of large noon shade behind the creaky
shed. Tall lily clumps decide to shrink their
giant spiders further and further
in the grass. Doves and Wrens remember
the seed trail broadcast the day before.
Sun remembers distant treetops. Lawn
chairs recall none of this. Till now it
was not here. Their cups of tea and spots
of shade see only their present.

158
Friday, June 7, 2013

The low pitched sonic boom of all-night
rain burrows through caverns of black. Black
woods. Black yards. Black clouds. Black sky. It flings
its bottomless pocket of marbles
down onto the deck. And the roof. From
both ends, its flashfloods flood the street in
raging runaways. They converge in
cascades at the bridge's wall. They spout
into the black stream and mount the black
banks. Like pale spots of fleeting time—from
time to time—the clouds flicker and pulse.
The flickers—from time to time—grumble.
The blackboard sky wipes its slate. Black clouds. Black
yards. Black woods. Low pitched boom. Black rain.

159
Saturday, June 8, 2013

Like kids in a car's backseat, the hit
and miss tussle between a threat of
rain and blare of sun skirts a fine line.
Their indecisiveness holds no beef
with the towel soft cool of waking air.
A late morning hit-miss shaft of quick
sun splashes bold shadows across the
lawn and pavement. Like a marquee beam,
its direct hit cuts straight through the gloom
along the stream bank by the culvert
and, spilling down tissue puffs of sky,
it floodlights the Hydrangea in an
eruption of blue. Like a girl at a
dance solo, the bush steals the whole show.

160
Sunday, June 9, 2013

The hurricane drives its six-engine
diesel up the coast. Three hundred miles
behind its tight eye, loaded cargoes
roll. In bands that stretch far west and north,
its swill of warm Gulf water rides in
hydra headed paunches. The hydrant
pressured clouds bust open and gush. The
afternoon struggles to keep its head
up. Streets crest into streams. Lawns swamp down
with clogged storm drain refuse and leaves. The
creek's slim meander engulfs a lake
whose whirlpool churns branches and trash. Now
knows no way to slam the brakes. It stares
from its window and rides itself out.

161
Monday, June 10, 2013

Groggy pre-dawn air wakes hungover
from its drunken binge. Muggy mist blurs
its puffy eyes. Dank wet odors reek
of quiet urine and slept in clothes.
No pelting downpours pummel headaches
inside its head, only the dripping
dark of the air and the creek's timid
lullaby. It's the hum a child back
in its bed after a party went
too long. In each right place are favorite
toys: frogs—owls—kingsnakes—and overhead,
Starling nests. Content it waits a mug
of coffee and towel to sit with its
song on the stone damp of the porch steps.

162
Tuesday, June 11, 2013

Thirsty sun's mid-afternoon tongues are
on the prowl. They lick tomato
skins into timid blushes. They suck the
shriveled squash blooms into tiny knobs.
They lap the spongy damp from potted
soil and drive the vein red streaks of beet
leaves up like stretching wings. Their cat purr
scratchy tongues lave the sweating trickle
on the neck and search the membranes that
softly line the backside of the ears.
Tongues open out like seductive hands
to kneed the oils of their warmth into
the spine and head. Surfaces murmur
with ravishment and stupefaction.

163
Wednesday, June 12, 2013

The shower comes and goes like a bad
performance with a single clap that soundly
shows the neighborhood's disgust. The sun's
disguise never fully masks its face.
It knows how shoddy the affair is
likely to turn out. It expects a
bad review. As if a mangle in
a cleaners that stretches three blocks jerked
straight uphill, the pavement spurts heavy
steam. The heat scarcely misses a stride
as cars go and come, except over
across the ridge of trees, fading layers
of the rainbow, like a critic's brief notes,
keep right on with the show's finale.

164
Thursday, June 13, 2013

Like a grandma's sloppy scrub of a
boy's face and peck on his cheek, showers
gush fast and rough. They quickly dry. While
clouds towel clean the sky, the rainbow holds
court in the east. Decked out in circus
attire of violet onion skin
ribbons, pumpkin orange sashes, and silk
saris molten with spun rubies and
burnished gold, sunset pounces the west.
In florid tights and head plumes, its grace
balances high wire headstands. Its leaps
float from wide trapezes. As the show's
drum rolls, applause and spotlight shut down,
colored scraps strew the horizon floor.

165
Friday, June 14, 2013

Dire sirens should broadcast a warning
before this phalanx of heat rears up
its snarl in confrontation with the
day's noon. Halted, the tracks scarcely make
it down the five front steps from the door.
Desire to drive withers on the vine.
Silence is stealth like the fumes from cars
boiling up into unbreathable stew.
The tracks turn back. The blue quartz blaze of
a Skink darts up the wall. The door pulls shut
and drapes pull an illusion of cool
down around the room's shadows. Up the
hill where illusions have no trees to
hide them, asphalt is licorice glue.

166
Saturday, June 15, 2013

With its departing mists, amber dusk
wanders across the dinner hour's
shower, the way aromas drift their
savory steam in a warm kitchen:
turmeric stew and saffron rice and
backing gourd-shaped halves of butternuts.
The kinesthetic air pulses with
color's body. It throbs in moisture's
glow. Buried in dark roiling billows, sun
is helpless to burn through with departing
shafts. The clouds scoop down dark wide bands of
starless sky. They snuggle in their warm
saturations across roofs and trees.
Their lullabies start with moans of owls.

167
Sunday, June 16, 2013

The late afternoon view across the
road does not consider itself a
view. It holds no distinction between
viewer and viewed, being neither. *Why,*
it asks, *am I called a view?*
Why me and not the house opposite
with eight old cars stranded in its wide
clay-beaten grass-barren gravel yard?
Nevertheless, the roadside woods are
spotted with Silk Trees in their first day's
full bloom. The feather-fine clusters lie
on stacked ferny leaves like porcelain
curios as the western sun shafts
strike them with tremolos of coral.

168
Monday, June 17, 2013

Sunrise rises elsewhere when the back is
turned. Facing up the hill's four houses
each with three canvasses hanging
in window frames across its face, sun-
rise faces its gallery of large
acrylics. Each erupts its glowing
variation of pinks and yellows,
where minute to minute, bands of blue
shift into marines, azures and aquas.
Swallowing the yellows, floating the
pinks, clouds sweep long striations from edge
to edge. As the gallery longs to
hold a photo's now, behind the turned
back, the full sun wipes each image off.

169
Tuesday, June 18, 2013

The parting waters of small clouds stand
aside as sun rolls its blaze forward
to the engulfing brink. As the hour
elongates into stretched suspense, sun hangs
poised to tumble over. The bowlful
of pink-edged puffs and regal blue take
no notice. Rewarded for its patience,
imperceptibly day's sweeping length
forms broad striations in lilac and
orange. With savoring sips that linger
as slow as sunset, wine glasses on
the deck drain the hour's piquancies.
They vow not to forget. *The print of
this now will not fade*, they say.
They fade.

170
Wednesday, June 19, 2013

Trampled underfoot by the steady
march of rain—trounced with mud—in backyard
seclusion, three Stargazer Lilies
decide to take hold of the noon sun
and open their shut up lids. They wink through
grit of clay. They grapple through mats of
shadow. They push back the creep of ground
ivy. The mower's fell swath swerves in
an instant's nick. It gives wide berth.
Clipped—rinsed from a trickling hose—brought in—
tucked in a kitchen tumbler, they stretch
wide pristine pale raspberry star-burst
poignancies. Shy garnet freckles blush.
Stamens glint with tiny garnet flames.

171
Thursday, June 20, 2013

Like balls hanging in tight rows on each
twig and bough to trim a tree, small hard
peaches glow in lime and rouge and sun
bright orange. The squat tree's maladroit limbs
long to stretch high and embrace the high
east light. Their small crinkly leaves long to
sing high notes in the key of green but
plentitude and lavishness share a
different scheme. Fruit conspires to pull the
tree earthwards. Brokeback branches stretch and
bleed their sap's shiny amber blood. Large
black ants nibble at the gum-hard scabs
and sun's daily deep massage weighs down
each fruit with succulence and juice.

172
Friday, June 21, 2013

The kitchen window, hands washing last
night's wine glasses in warm suds while
coffee steams, wants to recall the vow
to the indelibility of
sunset. The vow holds vacancy as
wide as grief, for its out-flowing light
flowed out. Morning shadows entice the
window's new found infidelity. They own
half the shaggy grass. Crisp and sparkly
with dew, the other half is kiwi
green. Free of promises, Chickadees
twitch and skip from shade to light and back.
Both halves of lawn join voice and command:
Drink your cup, we want our fresh mow now.

173
Saturday, June 22, 2013

The shortest night procrastinates in
ritardandos of half light. Quenching
down gulp on white gulp of reflected
vanished sun, the super moon flares
the eastern sky. Its large stillness takes
control. Sidewalks and patios glow
in pass-me-down refractions. Birds nest
in hushed coverts. Tree domes stand blacker.
Basking in serenity, its ride
across the sky carries each minute's
now into the next—implacably.
On the patio table, the words
of an open book seek no porch light
or candle to tell their silent tale.

174
Sunday, June 23, 2013

Hardly noticed, moon trails behind sun's
flamboyant departure, so when the
vermilions snuff their flickering wicks,
the sky top is shocked with the big white
of it. Shadows spread in haste, as the
whiteness rains a mist-like scrim across
the black stick-puppet silhouettes of trees.
Already they're doing their stick-puppet
rumba with tip-top arms. Inaudible
drums and marimbas have brought Cuban
beaches into the yard. Listen. And
into the neighbor's yards. Both sides. And
all the yards—as far as a second
floor balcony and porch chair can see.

175
Monday, June 24, 2013

Pyramid layers of the Silk Tree
cake are frosted in Calamine pink
and limeade green. They glow in midday
light. They shimmer in the noontide breeze
like crystallized sugar. Direct blasts
of trumpet-shrill sun are powerless to
send the layers running into puddles
of ooze and sticky syrup. The breeze
is powerless to scatter the creamy
tufts down into sidewalk splats. Like flies
at an outdoor buffet, erratic
Starlings dart about the branches. Their
shadows dart about mottles of
twinkling shadows that lace the grass.

176
Tuesday, June 25, 2013

Pre-dawn sweats beneath sheets rumpled with
too many covers and too little
air. Parked car hoods and windows sweat. Splashed
with clover, the lawn sweats. Deck slats sweat.
The all-night hose nozzle dribbles a
small marsh. Bare feet on the deck aim toward
the faucet to turn it off. Surprised,
a plump Green Frog skims across the deck.
Ineptly it dives into the grass
below. The faucet knob twists the wrong
way. The hose leaps with a cold gush at
the t-shirted back. It spasms with
laughter. Inept bare legs dive across
the wet grass. Mud slicked, their butt flops flat.

177
Wednesday, June 26, 2013

"And lord how they soar" neither blasphemes
nor reveres. Midday the barrage of cars
vanishes and heat irons pavements. The window
points out two Turkey Vultures bobbling
in the front lawn like wind-up fairground
curios. They twist the sheen of their
long necks as they beak the dead rabbit.
They point their throats to swallow. Pink globs
string from their beaks. Their neck sheens glint like
tinfoil. The window can't stop staring
out. Such awkwardness in birds. Listen.
A cyclist blasts the sound barrier
and streaks past. First one then the other's
wingspan takes flight "And lord how they soar."

178
Thursday, June 27, 2013

The mower climbs back into the shed
and a half-empty stale sack of corn
scatters the neat lawn. Now busy black
late afternoon splotches dapple it.
As ravishing scents lure them down, Starlings
swoop from the creek bank woods. Unlike Wrens
or Robins, who know the habits of
the watchful windows, each shadow on
the kitchen pane gusts the Starlings up
like a seine cast out to sea. They dive
back, each kernel snared. Frenzy provokes
short-lived, beak squawking, wing-boxing spats.
They strip an hour clean. They fly off.
The grass lies alone, naked and mown.

179
Friday, June 28, 2013

Night's cool-down's a temporary fix.
Early heat invades. Honeysuckles
coil snake-bark vines around the trunk of
the holly tree. They dangle yellow
clumps. Where sun bakes a bare clay spot in
the lawn, Miner Bees flock out in the
grass. They scamper in soundless frenzy
from their hole and back. Sworn to mutual
aid, Honeysuckle blooms enfold
the interloping bees into their
interloping bosoms and, while vines
snare the fence and tighten invasive
strangleholds, bees spread promiscuous
kisses in return from bloom to bloom.

180
Sunday, July 21, 2013

Don't stop looking just to take sides with
the wriggling cricket. You see victim
then. Look simply. This thread is a line
taking a slow walk around itself
to view every side. It sees angles
and arcs. It sees interstices. Its
eloquence wavers in the light. Its
journey forth and back snares crickets but
can't snare breezes. Hello! a breeze can't
snare it. Its spider hangs from her legs
as motionless as a swimmer's deep
breath before her dive. Dare to trace the
line to its source. Dare not look away.
Stillness to watch is yours—to wait, hers.

181
Sunday, June 30, 2013

Moon is a late riser. Darkness has
pulled thick velvet drapes across the trees.
Aimless light escapes across space from
the stars' atomic blasts. Through a gap
between branches and the tall window,
a solo white star's unintended
light falls across a sleeping face. Without
intention the body heaves over
and a naked arm hangs to the floor.
Beneath a starlit shift of lid and
lash, eyes dance their shiftless dream. Were one
eye to open, it would peer into
the long stream of photons whose light years'
waves crest here and crash down on this shore.

July Journal

1
Monday, July 1, 2013

Despite uptown's glowing aureole,
from all five edges, white stars bloom.
Their irrepressible brightnesses
flicker and sing. Moon rises up late
in their daisy field sky. Its half slice
sings a song as white as theirs. It rides
the disregard of self-containment.
Drawing deep breaths through open windows,
it watches neither eyes asleep nor,
tracked through labyrinths, the dreamer's quest.
Where daisies call their distances
across the universe, the moon climbs
overhead to perch its pinnacle.
Sunrise finds it there to chase away.

2
Tuesday, July 2, 2013

The half upturned kayak of a half
slice moon is slowly sucked beneath the
tree-top waves that frolic darkly on
the western rim. Across the sky the
bully sun is elbowing its way
through the banks of clouds. Knowing well its
aim is high and ruthless with its skin
abusing scorch, the apple tree stands
like a pacifist, unperturbed and
stoical. Its lima green golf balls
dangle from its drooping spider-arm.
The fruits are golf ball hard. No kin to
haste, their skins and flesh soak up the scorch.
Their greed for sun is unquenchable.

3
Wednesday, July 3, 2013

Into the respite from the wind-throw
burst of rain, trees drip down through muggy
light. Dusk dangles a thin gauze haze.
In tropic heaviness along the
surging creek, trees glow in agate greens.
Starlings dart about in the amber
shafts of light. Tucked demurely between
tall Sycamores and Oaks, the Fringetree's
creamy old man's beards wobble and sway
full bloom. Skimming blossoms here and there,
two snowflake butterflies dance circles
around each other. A Lightning Bug
blinks in the gloom. As amber respite
holds, another blinks. And another.

4
Thursday, July 4, 2013

Sun's setting post-mortem wakes up the
high-rise horizon lights with confetti
sprays and muffled pops. Like moon-spill on
ripples across a lake, they recede and
evaporate in the indigo
dark. Bursting with spurts of puckering
flavor, from time to time, silver spears
sail up to blast parachuting drifts
of mirth. In private contemplation
the barefoot deck chair keeps its vigil.
In honor of how this present is
tense with an odd annual display
of transience and community,
it eats sliced peaches and sips iced tea.

5
Friday, July 5, 2013

A glass half full of good Shiraz sits on
the deck rail long after the other glass,
the conversation and four bare feet
have moved inside. The time has come when
mosquitoes, no longer pacified
by heavy air, hunger for blood, and it
has gone. The sun's last shafts strike garnets
ablaze in the wine where two sluggish hornets
flail. A small slug and its mica trail
inch up toward the lip. The candle, sput-
tering to a wad of dried pink slime
like chewed discarded bubble gum, dies
on the redwood table in its cup.

6
Saturday, July 6, 2013

Heat strokes the waist high tomato plants
weighed down already with lima-green
balls. Embarrassed they understand that
to perk-up they need a good early
morning dousing. As the shadows pull
back and the sun hits harder, this is
their best hope. Their leaves hang limp. A King-
snake drifts along the chicken wire fence
to find a warm dry patch of grass to
stretch out her full black length and set up
watch. The oblivious hose hangs coiled
on its back wall hook. The porch's door
does not slide open to this now—whose
names are *expectancy* and *waiting*.

7
Sunday, July 7, 2013

The late morning shower picks up its
skirts and scurries off to find a new
county to douse. Like aromas that
push through oven steam, sun breaks out, fresh,
yeasty and full of body. In their
wake, flouncing skirts fling ruby sequins
down on plum tree leaves. Sapphire sequins
spark Hydrangea petals. Peridot
sequins gleam in the grass. Out of the
cloudbank riding off in the sky, like
five well-spaced silver geese, one silent
jet after another floats out from
the dark mound. Afterthoughts of their roars
sink to earth in dim belatedness.

8
Monday, July 8, 2013

Like an underwater breath ready
to explode, sky holds the sunrise tight
below its belt. As if white were the
sum of all expectancy, from each
far side, sky splats vast runny swathes of
whitewash across the blinding eastern
wall. As darkness blankets streets and lawns,
it mutters warnings to itself. Sky
exhales. Sun carves up gloom into sharp
long shadow edges which, like run-off
water ebbing down to the stream, shrink
inch by implacable inch. Sunlight
inundates the shade. Its conquest is
the whole matter that matters now.

9
Tuesday, July 9, 2013

Fourteen days away on business else-
where, sunset is back at work pouring
spot-lit white across all the backside
windows of each hill slope house. Inside, floors
and walls are puddled. The puddles shift
and shrink. Outside, the saturated
trees blaze in Boric Acid shimmers
and green flames. Sun's white glare slithers down.
Branch by branch, emerald flames flare up. The
topmost limbs prance against the dimming
sky. The way music fades in movie
scenes, the dazzle swallows itself up.
Mute strings modulate through somber chords
of gray. Stillness rides the overtones.

10
Wednesday, July 10, 2013

Sky pours into its bowl a thin gruel
of afternoon and heat and haze. The
mix ferments and bubbles. Oxygen
sucks in. Gassy fumes pour out. The bowl
inverts to spread a smoky beery
staleness. Flatulence oozes over
lawns and up on porches. It fills small
useless shadows squeezed around tree roots.
With slow deliberations it sucks
life from passing time till lifeless hours
lie lifelessly for hours. Heaving up
one plastic bag-stuffed dumpster after
the next, garbage trucks grind down the street.
Their well-soured rantings feel right at home.

11
Thursday, July 11, 2013

Worn with frumpy ease, saturation
is the morning's favorite pet name. Sky
bulges with the murk of bulky clouds.
Air, on the verge of tears, perspires with
steamy dank. Soil gasps beneath stifling
crab grass and doughy mud. It stunts the
okras. It chokes the squash plants and holds
them down. The creek is throttled with trash
and branches. As if it had no wish
to fix itself to go out to be
presentable—or clunkiness were
now the latest fad—morning drags its
wrapped blanket up to the edge of noon.
Its night sweats sweat out the entire day.

12
Friday, July 12, 2013

*Reach beneath our high noon leaves. Braise your
wrist against their beard stubble. Smell their
weedy herb stains on your sweat. Twist us—
one by one—from our goose neck stems. Small
lopsided ones with pale orange streaks. Large
round ones that rest their smooth scarlet orbs
in your palm. The ones with hard bubbly
ridges at their stem ends. One by one—
place us in the plastic colander
in the grass. As you lift the white plastic,
where two long plump cucumbers and the
mound of us lies, raise us to your nose.
Our whiffs of stored warmth float across your
eyes. Our juice awaits your lips and tongue.*

13
Saturday, July 13, 2013

Steam's heavy breath exhales from the
concrete driveway and stone path across
the yard. Honeysuckle air hangs in dense
warm residue from early morning
showers. It's a bad aerosol spray
freshener—that fails to freshen.
It's a cheap cologne dashed across an
adolescent boy's chest with too much
élan. Like limp car wash rags, drying,
the vine drapes across the kennel fence
slats where a pair of doggie-smelling
wet dogs lies with noses at the gate—
panting. Broadcast to the yard, splatters
of furry and orange musk hurl insults.

14
Sunday, July 14, 2013

Transforming pinkish green to scarlet
and sour firmness into lavish
juice, the time of night works its magic.
Stars in their contented ignorance
neither watch nor turn away. The moon
simply slices down the western rim
and vanishes. Alone on separate
stems, tomatoes are plumping themselves
up for dawn and dew. They are early
risers. Decked in all their readiness,
coyness is a bold disguise to hide
their unrestrained seductions. Wrapped in
soft nocturnal glows, *Watch out,* they sing,
we'll debauch and over-brim your chin.

15
Monday, July 15, 2013

The consoling shower departs—turns back—
smiles—waves reluctantly—and saunters
off. Amber is its afterglow. Two
rabbits shiver in their damp fur shawls.
Clover leaves are beaded with water
like rinsed lettuce. As if perched in down nests,
the rabbits crouch in the thick grass.
With bovine ruminations over
cud, their contented jaws grind back and
forth. Black eyes stare out each side. A last
regretful shrug of droplets and the
shower evaporates into the sun's
bugle blaring wide sinking eye. Dark
blue tucks down night across the big sky.

16
Tuesday, July 16, 2013

As the thermometer climbs its tube
so does day; first into sunlight, then
dry air, then torch blue sky. Afternoon
climbs higher. Dryer. Three hawks scour the
lofty blue clarity. Afternoon
breathes in elations of an end to
rain. With each exhalation, it knows
also jitters of young Sparrows that
dart up and down the trees. They ply their
busy craft beneath hawk scan eyes. Each
new now of day's moment by moment
climb flashes back and forth shining its
double bright blade. Jitters. Elations.
The whet's urgency of each is keen.

17
Wednesday, July 17, 2013

North, just past the anxious ridge of trees
rippling and teetering higher and
higher, clouds stack tanks of water one
atop the next. Orange splotches the murk
of black impenetrabilities.
Their turbulence is like cogs of a
gyrating gothic tower clock. Some
grind methodically. Some whir like
rushing mills. Thrashing trees come nearer
blowing a new now before them. Trash
and plastic bags fly up like kites. They're
whisked as high as trees just as one tall
cloud's black maw spews lightening. The watching
opened door counts each silent second.

18
Thursday, July 18, 2013

Unimpeded noon braises roofs and
pavements with its iron skillet. Like
abruptly modulating chords, the
Oriole's sleek wings greet the buoyant
face of the Sunflower. Their yellows
are a meeting of kindred yang and
ying. From drooping petals, loosened seeds
reach up to find the prying beak. The
fluttering wings hover with strength to
pluck the morsels free. The bird sails off
to the Junipers to crack apart
its prizes. Obedient to sun's
commands, the blossom's head contorts its
afternoon sundial neck back around.

19
Friday, July 19 2013

Beyond the sultry gate, evening picks
its way through warm rambling shadows. It
wears no shirt and knows no sun block is
required by the woods' illusion
of permanence. The dulcet muffled
modulations of this now listen.
Dim orange light guards cautious steps over
rotting fallen logs and wiry swirls
of thorn brambles. Leaf-filled stump holes have
set small trickster pranks. Just beyond the
moments' failing gray, a pair of Hawk
chicks bickers and shoves. The adults watch
the half-grown young tuck heads down into
the nest and fold wings across their backs.

20
Saturday, July 20, 2013

In their siesta rest beneath wide
umbrella leaves, swollen, palm-sized and
splotched with streaks of inexplicable
amethyst, juice plumped dugs hang down.
Leaves itch with pastiness. The spread of
leaves enwombs a cove of cooler air.
Stand inside. Between clusters of small
hard figs, ripe swollen dumplings protrude.
There, inside, reach up. As if to pluck a
blossom easily bruised, lift each fruit
from its stem. Don't squeeze. Don't drop. One by
one, place them in the glass bowl. The rain
and the sun deliver births into
sweetness. Carry them in. Chill them. Dine.

21
Sunday, July 21, 2013

Clouds bump around the thunder dark sky.
Light's pulses from smothered timpanis
flicker across the tops of surging
trees. Like black island pools, star speckled
patches shut and open amid the
frenzy. As if it were a thunder
flash itself—more solid, less fleeting,
almost round, glowing iridescent white—
the moon flares wide in interstices
of open sky. It slowly mounts the
shifting ladder. It ducks behind
each swell of clouds. It opens its full
face inside depths of placid black. Star
speckles twitter in silent accord.

22
Monday, July 22, 2013

Sunset wilts slowly behind the bank
of busy dark trees. Already in
full white stride the moon roars in, in bold
control of the eastern sky. Stars dare
not compete. Like a small tug ahead
of a huge lit barge, the twittering
light of an airplane guides its silent
arrow above the pregnant wholeness,
then, severing the umbilical,
moves apart. Moon needs no guidance. It
knows its way. From park trails, bus stops,
porches and cars held hostage at red
traffic lights, its brazen confidence
attracts swarms of admiring eyes.

The Present Tense

23
Tuesday, July 23, 2013

Early afternoon's minutes dangle
precariously on raw green pears.
Marauding squirrels leap down from slim
Hickories like crows swooping to road kill.
Tugging each pear from its stem, knife teeth
incise chunks of sour nut-hard flesh.
Inviting the ants to come dine, the
wounded pears plunge to the grass. Their falls
are dead with the thuds of cracked drum heads.
Fermenting into soft cidery
brown spots, their relentless unconcern
joins wounded fruit from yesterday—and
the day before. By dawn, they'll sweat
with cool dew. For now time's all a waste.

24
Wednesday, July 24, 2013

Shadows open their eyes. Dawn whispers
in. Fence-leaping deer drift through the shade
to gorge drunken breakfasts of rotting pears.
Absorbed in their business, they wear the
dew-crisp aura of hush. Darkness pales.
The yard smiles in agreement. When the
screen door slides, six tails perk. Twelve ears
twist. As if awakened, lean silent
legs turn and float across the far-back
fence, fading their dream, tan into tan,
between the dim trees. Morning readies
itself for the business of day with
humming mud hornets. They suck pear rot.
Files of ants scurry into the mash.

25
Thursday, July 25, 2013

The fig's shadowy undertones call to
be unburdened of this day's ripeness.
Clover heads reel in the gold shimmer
of lazy bees. Plain to see. They say:
Step elsewhere, not here. The shade thick late
afternoon's damp grass offers covert
asylum to guerrilla bands of
mosquitoes. Their pin head striped bodies
aim stealth bomber darts. Their silent wings
hover beneath sightlines of watchful
eyes. They play ancient blood sports. Bare calves
confront their offensive strategies.
In consternation, ankle veins kick
them off. Too late, indignity flares.

26
Friday, July 26, 2013

Noon's strained ozone sucks air from lawns and
lungs. It wears the asphyxiation
of the inside of hot air balloons.
Butterflies drift yellow sails from one
lavender tuft to the next. Toward the
cruel overbearing sun, Hibiscus
scarlet stars raise their screaming throats. Their
yellow tonsils stand erect and like
a dart board's green dart, a Hummingbird
slams in. The films frame freezes midair.
It sips sugar yellow sweetness with half
its body down inside. The film re-
starts and the green spot vanishes on
the sheer whirring of invisible wings.

27
Saturday, July 27, 2013

The sunset squinies into penny
small incendiary eyes. Direct
hits hurt. Like incandescent sheets of
ice across roof tiles, yellow-white boils
its sinking flare. Long lean parodies
of shadows emaciate themselves.
Sky retains its blue in darkened pools.
Arriving and departing vapor
trails widen in wakes of carmine—gold—
lavender. They are *sotto voce*
flutes and oboes piping quietly
above the trombone and tuba march
down into the horizon. Half-flared
peacocks melt to blue oblivion

28
Sunday, July 28 2013

Beneath boisterous frog choir rehearsals,
night spawns tiny inconveniences.
Back in the woods, half drowned water-logged
old tires swarm while nearby the wheelbarrow's
stagnant green water swims with squiggles.
Their wee genetics tick off quick nights
of metamorphosis. Their tiny
black-white Asian tiger stripes plan next
week's itineraries for muggy
afternoons of sniffing out neck sweat
and backs bent over bush bean clumps. Their
hypodermics plan attacks. For welts
to accost an hour with itching, their
codes already know where best to strike.

29
Monday, July 29, 2013

Beneath the window, the Butterfly
Bush stretches spider arms. Lavender
spikes wave at the late morning's dry breeze.
Breeze purrs with its warm fur. From time to
time like random thoughts, somnolent cars
mosey down the hill. Unhurried in
the prescience of now, one—then a pair—
black Swallow Tailed Butterflies flutter
down from the sky. One—then another—
and another—four Monarchs join them.
Arpeggios and syncopations
tap and touch the bush. With wings pulsing,
they rest. Unhurried, one by one they
flutter into the sky. Air is light.

30
Tuesday, July 30, 2013

Where the road dips to the creek, silver
whispers of fog unroll across the
yards. Higher up the slope, lawns are dark
and naked. It spreads its carpet of
gossamer light in the gentlest of
pale ankle-high ripples. Driveway cars
stand inside their hunkered frames. Streamlets
like tear-stains trickle down their window
glass and trunk lids. Pre-dawn sky is clear
and low. It draws its spatter of bright
flecks down to brush the black tree tops. Like
wraiths, two does and two half-grown fawns slide
through shadows across the sloshing creek.
Theirs is the gentlest of silences.

31
Wednesday, July 31, 2013

Rattling down the hill with sideswiping
shark jaw, tractor and mower mutilate
the mid-afternoon calm. Paucity
of traffic tells its big brazen lie.
As it grinds past, regurgitated
pabulum of weed shreds and wet juicy
grass spews the roadside in its wake. The
hay fresh smell is garnished with chopped trash:
sliced aluminum, paper, plastic
cups, Styrofoam boxes. Jangling the
windows, the din reaches its fullest
crescendo, then climbs the next sloping hill.
This now's afternoon calm is gone. Like a
relaxing muscle cramp, noise abates.

August Journal

213
Thursday, August 1, 2013

Hot late afternoon chokes air from throats
like the bark-thick wild Wisterias
choke the old creek-side Willow Oaks. Their
vines snake tight cords up to tall limbs
and pontoon eager tentacles high
across into Crabapple and Peach
tree canopies. Air's tentacles wrap
rubber bands tightly around each strained
lung. As it orders out the evening
horde of Tiger Striped Mosquitoes, heat's
drill sergeant sadism suffers no
mercy. Clinging to the tight range of
the shed's shadow, two rabbits creep to
the clover that hugs the dying stump.

214
Friday, August 2, 2013

Noon's fried air seethes. With engines panting
their spent excitement of escape, a
pair of pit bulls trots up the road. They
veer from the middle lane to poke at
fast food bags and Styrofoam soda
cups hurled from car windows to the road-
side grass. Even small shadow islands
bear the brunt of the sun. A motor-
cycle roars down the hill. The midriff
girl hugging the guy's back streams a blond
mane from beneath her helmet. The dogs
dart through back yards to the porch they know.
They cower. The air is stretched thin by
exhaust fumes. It tires fast and breathes hard.

The Present Tense

215
Saturday, August 3, 2013

As through a covered bridge, streetlights spread
intermittent pools along the tall
wide-spanned Willow Oak-arched street. The street
strides the shallow hill past porches set
back behind dark yards. Like splats of strange
up-gusted black snow, or dark autumn
leaves flitting down and up small breezes,
bats vacuum through the warm night air. They
dive at moths. They dart and swerve to scoop
their gullets full of mosquitoes. They
snatch sluggish midflight midges. As the
light peels night vision eyes, the dim street
transmogrifies itself into zigzaging
mercurial trigonometries.

216
Sunday, August 4, 2013

As small as cat slaps, midmorning air
paws the leaves that ridge the tree tops. High
and sluggish in their waking, a few
Cicadas there and here begin to
contract their tymbal cavities like
brittle grinding bones. Their sounds are like
violins stalking into their chairs one
by one long before the conductor's
wand lifts to call for hush—then falls. Males—
one by one—warm to dusk's far away
crescendo of grand stampedes. This now
is indolent. Its small rattle of
bones surrounds the breezes with hush. Surrounds
trees with inevitability.

217
Monday, August 5, 2013

Afternoon pants uncontrollably.
Scummed over with mosquito larvae,
its water dish is low. As okras'
spear-tipped fingers stiffly beckon to
monarchs and chameleons, heat hangs in
harsh layers. The stream is almost dry.
Sluggish pools, shadowed below tree roots
dangling their thick calves over the bank,
swarm with black darts of frog spawn. The heat
paw-pads around and around the dirt
radius of its ten foot rusty
chain. It thirsts for shade and whimpers a
somnolent dirge. Dirt's baked adobe
wears thin cracks of fine heirloom china.

218
Tuesday, August 6, 2013

They arrive overnight from wood stands,
backyards and gardens. Stretched across the
distant street-end, their accord is one
voice. Above the tree line along the
high-strung wires of the single file
of voltage raging towers that stride
beside the tracks—as the molten sun
rolls up—rows of countless gleaming black
Starlings rise and fall back to the wires.
They are getting acquainted. The year's
young meet their elders. They tell of Hawks
and how to confuse them. They discuss
the best breakfast spots. They plan for joint
flocking swirls and massive skyfalls.

The Present Tense

219
Wednesday, August 7, 2013

The mower plunges through shower wet
late morning grass. Mulch dribbles out in
pasty clumps. Where the creek right angles
over small rapids to lose itself
in the woods, along the back stretch of
yard and slippery mud, swirling blades
ride over clay mounds and dark frog holes.
In swift splats, they escape and leap high
into the water. As the mower
pushes past, gouges of fresh deer hooves fill
with small puddles. Its mandibles aimed,
a Deer Fly strikes through jeans and sweaty
long sleeves. Outraged burning welts flare up.
Ignoring them, swirling blades grind on.

220
Thursday, August 8, 2013

Afternoon shade sucks draperies of
humidity from pools of dark shade
up into indolent canopies.
In their lofts Cicadas crackle with
the dry persistence of small machines.
Their rapid snare drum brushes twirl
in limp vibrations of heavy air.
The ear's horizon stretches far down
the creek cut where on their unseen nest,
quarrelling adolescent Hawks caw
like disgruntled crows. Far above their
ears' horizons, the parents ride the
sky and watch. Afternoon is hammock dazed—
mosquito wary—and iced tea glad.

221
Friday, August 9, 2013

In dark Conch shell swirls of shadows,
a thousand twangling instruments sing.
Midnight bends its ruptured ear. Loops of
minimalist percussion entwine
the air from all ten sides. From tree bark
perches, Cicada castanets click and
clack their stereophonic calls to
calls from calls. The frogs' cabasa whirs
into the ear in ricocheting
flows and ebbs. The hoot-crack of an owl
slaps its drum skin with metronomic
clock-work. A weary dog's incisive
clave strokes, as if to rebuke the
owl, yelp from the stretched end of his chain.

222
Saturday, August 10, 2013

The sky lays dim slate above the trees.
Looming silhouettes breathe in blackness.
Air exhales cool damp silence. Stillness
in the trees echoes cool silence back.
A few lone Cicadas call from edge
to edge. Their erratic dry clicking
makes the shape of silence palpable
like, just before a song begins, breath's
intake holds the upbeat up. Out of
the silence, as awareness takes shape,
crossing by crossing, a train's bleak howl
approaches. Silence holds its breath. It
waits the train to pass the street end. It
forgets to breathe. It goes back inside.

223
Sunday, August 11, 2013

Noon sun toasts the driveway to a fine
sizzle. A Skink's feet luxuriate
on the heat of porch bricks. Its no-neck
slice of blue light darts down the crawl space
wall. In the cement cracks along the
side of the parked car, it laps up ants. It
lifts its no-neck head and, with regal
wave, waves it nose up at a sun
that broils the white cloudless sky. Like small
electric currents, its ritual
of homage twitches through every nerve.
It skitters back to the wall. A small
dry dollop of black excrement marks
the spot of its now—that now—is was.

224
Monday, August 12, 2013

Dusk wakes up into deep grottos of
Tourmaline and Jade. Air holds itself
captive to the amber light. Its eyes
sink into indolence. Its ears rise
to wrest control. Sounds describe its fourth
dimension. Dusk's ears are mesmerized
by nameless cornucopias of
crackles, chatters, clickings, buzzes, hums
and distant caws. They drink them up like
thirsty sponges. They imbibe pallets
of twangling flavors. On their nerves, they
gather vibrancies of textures: crisp,
hard, crinkly, crunchy, wafting, fallow.
Dusk's fourth dimension intones them all.

225
Tuesday, August 13, 2013

The sun's old fashioned irons take turns
sitting on the wood stove's hot bellied
glow, then pressing, like starched shirts, the stone
patio's polished granite, where the
cat's ginger pricks a judicious path
through grass patches that edge them. No bare
feet here. By four o'clock, mercury
takes a direct hit and declares one-
twenty degrees. Delighted, Skinks criss-
cross the stones in ant picnics and dry
whitish droppings. Afternoon is theirs.
Snouts aimed, they crane their necks, halt their tracks
and bask. Their tongue flicks rest on the dream-
hums of bees in near-by okra blooms.

226
Wednesday, August 14, 2013

Evening gathers up its colander of
crisp mantis-green okra pods. Its swift
wrist snaps each off. Nestled with them, lie
shiny cucumbers and a matched pair
of tomatoes. Setting its harvest on
the hammock net, sunset opens the
grand cotillion of puffed and flaring clouds.
Fuchsia foxtrots with a full bosomed
yellow matron. Burgundy sweeps gold
across a slender wisp's exited arms and
spins the sweet young thing high above his
lithe elegance. Horizon burns in
brassy blasts of orange. The colander
forgets to pick up and go inside.

The Present Tense

227
Thursday, August 15, 2013

The slant of early sun burns fast through
shadows, and streaks the lawn. The mower
spews out swathes of tangy grass mulch forth
and back. Like coffee steam, dew lifts puffs
from the shaggy slope waiting for its
predestined shearing. Cap and sun-block
pretend to help. As the snarl nears the
stream, frogs, arrow-quick and lean, leap from
their undercover blinds and splat the
water's bared chest. Roused from its morning
bask, a Box Turtle's overturned bowl
glints the shuttling light. The sun
goes right on fanning its blinding flame
higher. The mower jerks left and veers.

228
Friday, August 16, 2013

As sun taunts the horizon edge, clouds
bloom wide moorlands of rippling heather.
Hold your breath. They don't last. In shifting
kaleidoscopic acrobatics,
light and clouds are sly and shiftless. Streaks
shift up into billows. Vermilions
shift to creams and yellows. Striated
sheets of gray open into tucks and
folds. Nothing stays. Standing in firm bare
feet and dewy grass, each easy breath
inhales its own cloudscape, and as it
escapes into a gasp, each scape is
already something else. Sun's raw now
already rolls up a crimson head.

229
Saturday, August 17, 2013

Where it lies in its secret lair set
behind the trees and well behind the
row of houses, pomegranate blood
streaks the small lake in the woods. It is
split in two by the evening light. One
half is a mirror of motionless
upside down dark green trees with char black
trunks and branches. Shafts of sunset stab
through gaps between leaves to lacerate
the other half with dapples and raw
sanguine slices. Between the two, in
the silent borderland, six ducks drift
on their fluttering underwater
feet. Six heads bob in synchrony.

230
Sunday, August 18, 2013

A sojourner from a different sphere,
moon's ovoid swelling discus coasts high
above the afternoon. Afternoon
is busy with ozone's heavy press of
stillness. Its parched air sucks the spark from
lungs and sears drying sweat salt into
eyes. Eyes search the silent timeless sky
which revels in its distant bluish
milk emptied dry of any clouds. Eyes
search mats of mown mulch sloping the lawn
to the creek where small rapids carve small
clear water pools creased into the paste
of clay. The other sphere withholds its
full blue moonrise till another day.

231
Monday, August 19, 2013

Bridling its penchant for wind, all day
the offshore hurricane sends warnings
out and dispatches bands of steady
rain. With small island minds, Antillean
skies pelt neat inland lawns. The clouds part
company for unlikely swathes of
sweating sun. They join again and bathe
the street in hot tubs of rising steam.
Air, tangy with salt, whispers sultry
innuendos: *Wring your t-shirt out
into a cup. Take small sips. The water
tastes half ocean—like perspiration
on an upper lip.* Rain drives on and on
as the eye spines out to open waters.

232
Tuesday, August 20, 2013

A day—a night—four inches—dawn creeps
from steamy covers to find the sun
checking out the storm's mementoes. The
stream can't decide how to squeeze back down
between its banks. On lower branches
of thorn bushes, plastic bags, beer cans,
hamburger wrappers and half-limp "new
baby" pink balloons, show off. Choked with
mocha, water ripples across the
lower lawn. Where it slowly draws back,
washed out tulip bulbs with shredded leaves
spatter the mud grass. As if the lid
fell from the dumpster, a sour nameless
mix spills up into the bright fresh air.

233
Wednesday, August 21, 2013

Reckless to the unblocked dangers of
the sun's seductions, the late morning's
patient arousal lies face up in
the hammock. Like dry cat tongues, it licks
the skin of shirtless arms and swimsuit
legs summoning the skin to succulent
trickles of slow perspiration. Across the
closed eye's pupils, its breath paints fierce
red vistas with stabs of quick white. Its
kiss dries the salt of lips. Its patience
rubs deep and cradles with a parent's
arms. Its patience is of time that brooks
no closure to the *nowness* of this
now nor of the *hereness* of this here.

234
Thursday, August 22, 2013

Shadows from the streetlights whisper cool
kisses along the nape. They lick at
ear lobes. They tickle leg hairs. In the
ditch beside the road, grass is dark, wet
and shaggy. It calls to the stooping
silhouette: *Kneel low. Reach. Feel around.*
In the dark, wrapped in its plastic sheath,
the morning paper waits. Midges flit
around the groping wrists. They search in
vain. Knees decide instead to sip at
the mud. Like halos of cool breaths, damp
snuggles though the shirt. It stumbles to
stand. With glasses wiped, predawn fog walks
hand in empty hand back to the porch.

235
Friday, August 23, 2013

Thunderheads roil up in purple mounds
of dark excitement and then recede—
all day like monstrous bellows. Now, mid-
afternoon pressure builds the fevered
catharsis of a boil. It wears
the blackened robes of a tragic queen
whose horrid murders are about to
be exposed to a shrinking chorus
who wails in terror and awe. Dire
expectancy sends birds to dart in-
to shrubs and cats to slink beneath parked
cars. Heat seethes and day's steam swells higher.
Time holds hostage. Helpless against its
better judgment, the boil does not burst.

236
Saturday, August 24, 2013

Out of old myths of quest and wrath, tall
thunderheads march down from mountains
in the west and out across flood-plain
cities. Faster than newsman radar
warnings, they lash treetops until their
skirts whip up a frenzy of trollish
dancing. Droplets smack windows. Windows
slam shut. Angry threats knock about the
sky. Frantic wind-chimes clank. Door locks snap.
Crackling excitement in the lower
clouds, flashes fizzle like a scoreless
game of soccer and, as the ogres'
bullying exposes its bluster,
excitement packs up the rain and shrinks off.

237
Sunday, August 25, 2013

As the Sunflower's candelabra
arms burn out one curry yellow flame,
another flares. This noon's new blaze calls
out to bees. Black burly bubbles nudge
up and brush their wings against the sweet
fuzz. Where petals flitter to the ground,
the wide char of extinguished black wick
calls down the birds. An Oriole plucks
the wee black seeds. Upside down he cracks
it apart and drips shells. Like a spoke
torn loose, a long branch snaps. It hangs its
wound. Its abject tonsured head scrapes the
ground. Like rotted small black teeth, seeds fall
out. Bees and birds ignore its dismay.

238
Monday, August 26, 2013

Sky unfurls taut midnight gauze from rim
to rim. Smooth like mute violas, it
filters out the pricks of stars. The moon's
full cello's long solo bow notes gleam in the
reverberant haze. Above house roofs'
glow of soft ascending overtones,
its pristine white is sky's lone midpoint.
Lawns are mute sequins of crystalline
dew. Stillness in high dark trees regrets
no longings—expects no regrets. Theirs
is the silence of the blue moon's now.
Seeing midnight's dark negatives and
hearing its soundless dim counterpoints,
sleep is witless to its high bright now.

The Present Tense

239
Tuesday, August 27, 2013

Graciously exiting to let dry
air fill its wake and overflow the
sky, the moon sets early. Stars—even
in the city sky—pop out through black
infinity like Fireflies, while,
beneath the trees, Fireflies, orbit
like small stars. As midnight sets, hours
drift in its wake. Spreading in full view
across the skyscape above city
lights, with no thought yet of dawn, the slim
Perseid ribbons spawn silent flares
and streaks. The early runner's light stride
crowns a hill. Stopped in its tracks, the now
of running now sees what "countless" means.

240
Wednesday, August 28, 2013

Humid breath sweats from nights every pore
consorting with its tropic fever.
Yards contrive secret machinations.
The moon's a pale blur. Haze across
the low sky shuts the stars off. Acts of
darkness nestle inside the black that
hides low beneath the sweating trees. The
spongy soil rushes lawns into
fervid steroid growth. Scummy puddles
sprout mosquitoes that hide ankle-high
in grass laced with sprigs of small seeds.
They hover there in ambush for the
hapless mower who'll descend with dawn,
determined to reinstate order.

241
Thursday, August 29, 2013

A pair of khaki zigzagging darts
stabs at the creamy filaments of
tall Hibiscus blooms. Like children glad
their mother's come home, their scarlet stars
open wide arms to the sun. Humming
Birds take turns in erratic high-speed
aerobic routines. One flies off. The
other hovers. Both fly off. Both dart
back. The frenzy drives forward. Now, one
is gone. Abruptly, the other like
a child's finger—as still as a thought—
rests on an open-palmed leaf. Watching,
the window breathes tight. Snap. Gone. Scarlet
blossoms shine toward the sun. Sun moves on.

242
Friday, August 30, 2013

Merging and parting like voices that
sing madrigals *a cappella* in
white archipelagoes, small lotus
islands float across turquoise light. The
lawn plays games of dappled seek-and-hide
with shadows while the clouds' unmapped paths
mute and flash the sun. Coy breezes go
and come whispering secrets on
bare legs and arms. Shoes sit tossed on the
porch. Feet stroll through cool immaculate
grass beneath broad-leafed shade. While bees climb
through split-wide fallen fruit, high branched, the
afternoon serves its daily share of
figs plumped to swill warm juice down the throat.

243
Saturday, August 31, 2013

With near imperceptible pearl glow,
the quartzite sky's inverted counter
top rests just above the dark jade trees.
Like chords from distant English horns, the
sky's soft sheen is smooth and void. Heavy
cornucopias of leaves are still
and vacant too. From the stream bed, small
updraft breezes nudge low hung Sweetgum
leaves. They slowly jingle and twist on
their stems. On the culvert bridge where the
stream flows down, the street light reaches out
and tips the trembling leaves with neon
evanescent glints. Dusk breathes out its
final gasp and, unbemoaned, expires.

September Journal

244
Sunday, September 1, 2013

Like a well-breathed Burgundy, sunset's
slow slow amber purple afterglow
is flushed around its cheeks. It basks in
luxury and serenely refutes
that mosquitoes crave their wine blood too.
Dusk dozes in a silent deck chair
melody of drift. Its song summons
the sprawling chirps and crackles of frogs
from front and back yard woods. The keener
the daze tunes up its ears' attention
the more the expanding chorus sounds,
until, through distant tree canopies,
the purple horizon glows in dark
madrigalian antiphonies.

245
Monday, September 2, 2013

Heavy brownish clouds sweep their portents
up the sky from the far south to wipe
away the faltering late stars and
white hook moon. They embrace the sunrise
burst in huge magenta mounds. As they
watch in wary anxiousness, lawns wear
eerie lavender shadows. Strutting
in cavalier disregard up the
street, a pair of white pit bulls sashays
rumba buttocks and bulked biceps. Their
pre-dawn serendipitous loose gate
escape, they assume, abides its now
forever. The reckless dark sky says,
Forever's real name is never.

246
Tuesday, September 3, 2013

The Turkish Fig Tree hangs its purple
bells out in their orotundity
of juice. Late afternoon's humid warmth
laps sandy cat tongues on their skins. It
licks them into sweat. Skins split creases
for ants to swarm the cracks. Others split
apart oozing out their fuchsia hearts
and spleens. A sluggish orgy of drunk
entrails-hungry wasps celebrates.
Despite carnages, there and here, high
branch and low, ripeness bows down to
the tip-toe stretch of hands. The plastic
colander mounds above its rim. Warm
juice gushes mulled wine across the tongue.

247
Wednesday, September 4, 2013

As it lets go of the shadows' hold on
murkiness, the ebbing breath of night
brushes with cool soft fur. The shadows'
folds uncover varieties of
gray that reemerge in the pre-dawn
chorus that purrs like cats draped over
backs of sofas or on the sills of
windows. Meanwhile, like popcorn at full
throttle in a wire shaker on
campfire coals, the frogs have been firing
off all night. Shadow purrings and frog
cackles walk hand in hand along the
narrow balance beam toward a bleaching
sky that clears dawn's stage and sets its props.

248
Thursday, September 5, 2013

Their stalks snap. They overflow their wire
baskets. They sprawl on gangly arms. They
drape their coarse enervated giant
spider vines along the ground. Parched leaves
twist on nooses in the breeze. Like small
forlorn balls left on a derelict
Christmas tree thrown to the curb, along
the chaos of their spindly branches hard
Lima green tomatoes gleam in the
afternoon sun. *Don't pass us by*, they say.
We fry up nicely. Give us a try.
In a parallel cosmos, gnawing
the tannin-reek of Hickory nut husks,
squirrels go about their frantic chores.

249
Friday, September 6, 2013

Sunset hides behind a quilt of clouds.
The warm steady drizzle radiates
copper tinted light out across the
yard and through the evening trees. The wet
air glows. A stroll to the shallow stream
and plank bridge, then back to the back porch
deck, wears kelpy wet hair and a gauze
scrim on the glasses. The airy glow
sweats into the limp t-shirt. Along
the rim of the deck table hangs, like
miniature Chinese lanterns, a ring
of flawless teardrop pendants. At the
door, a shudder, like a shaking dog, runs
down and up the spine. A small spray falls.

250
Saturday, September 7, 2013

Like two kinds of time, trees reach out to
the wind marching down from the mountains
with sunset in its swirls of dark hair.
They are here—this here—as they bend and
snap back to flip their leaves upsided
as if no yesterday had weighed them
dry and limp. Those with pillar-like girth
know when also to lean—that other
time, which eyes guarding upstairs windows
have forgot. Eyes remember only
last year's tree crash across wires, the day
without power, hours of splintering
saws and their oily smoke marching through
windows flung open and reaching out.

251
Sunday September 8, 2013

Radiant through sheens of silk, light
breaks across wreckage from the wind's late night
tantrum. Dead branch claws and beams splotch the
yard like junk in a driveway from a
half-cleaned garage. Up the road behind
the house, a chain saw rattles the sun's
scouring hush. Fumes of oily smoke sneak
around parked cars, past the yard gate and,
as armloads of ant-swarmed limbs trudge to
the pile behind the fence, they lick at
sweaty neck and wrists. Figs distend hard
leather bulbs a week from ripeness and
ignore fumes and fuss. Their task is to
transmute green wax to purple velvet.

252
Monday, September 9, 2013

Clouds climb up their black billowing stacks
with engine pistons growling as if
to proclaim arrival. The only
party of welcome is the treetop
flurry of anxious leaves and the squall
of crows. The red soil with its blistered
dermatitis and cracked sores is too
parched to whoop it up or dance. The sun's
fright ducks its face behind scarves of dark
purple-orange—a color that calls eyes
up from their reading to gaze out the
window like timid kittens peering
from a hole cut in the side of an
overturned box. And the first splats land.

253
Tuesday, September 10, 2013

As if the blur of a dream pulled back
drapes on the way back from toilet to
bed and the north side windows spread their
panoramic sky like balconies,
midnight light pollution from uptown
shrinks to a small pool on the other
side. This side spreads an endlessness of
height all the way down to the treetops
across the road. Trees are dark. Sky is
black. Galaxies and suns bloom opal
white solitaries. One there. Three in
a line up here. Another elsewhere.
The proliferations of desert
skies are nowhere. Frugality is
this welcome's now. We take what we can.

254
Wednesday, September 11, 2013

Shining their oriole cartoon brass
horns, the Angel's Trumpet Tree blares from
its twelve foot-high silent perch, like a
Peruvian Baroque mural, down
to earth as if to raise the dormant
spirits of the dead. Lit in Lima
greens, its clusters of leaves aspire
to be comical giant holly sprigs.
The trumpets gape their hushed succulent
throats calling out to midnight: *Send us
your best moths. Let them have their dance.* The
afternoon sun stares, while with utter
disregard, draped in their own yellow
flames, Monarch Butterflies zig-zag past.

255
Thursday, September 12, 2013

Its truculent rumble and screeching
of jaws precede it. With a nimbus
of flies, its sour aura trails.
The waste compacter truck lands squarely
in front of the bin of bagged trash. Crab
pincers snugly hug the bin and lift
it overhead like a child too scared
to squeal or cry out. Belching a
rant of puking air, tossed to the grass
with lid splashed open, the bin gawks in
helpless disgust. Rescued, upended,
rolled to the back and doused with bleach, it
settles down. The humid breeze takes its
sweet time to clear the late morning air.

256
Friday, September 13, 2013

Lamentation for lost daylight al-
ready sneaks around corners just on
the periphery of starry nights.
It slinks on fox paws and drags half a
rabbit in its jaw, then startled, streaks
across the road when the mower drones
down the knoll coughing chartreuse stains on
the white vinyl fence. Figs burst open
and suckle fat wasps. Tomato vines
already change into sad swatches
of course rope. Night crawls through trees while its
shy rabbit friend nibbles clover clumps
left from the mower, and by the stream
frogs start their insomniac keening.

257
Saturday, September 14, 2013

Heat sticks to the skin and calls out to
mosquitoes to plant miniature
dollops of inflammation. Its breath
is humid like oven steam. Its weight
sinks down to deep lung sacks and stifles
oxygen. Between five fingered broad-
leaf shade, gaps aim direct hits of sun
at expectant figs. It plumps them up
like juicy dumplings. It unstitches
small seams in their purpling pink skin
to ooze out syrupy slow dollops.
Best served chilled and sliced with morning toast
and coffee, they stew sweetness. Their stems
drip milk that sticks on fingers. Pluck them.

The Present Tense

258
Sunday, September 15, 2013

Noon squats down on hot sweaty haunches
over the lawns and the road as if
its humidity were excrement.
The air rots and sours. Cars drive through
wondering if it will lift and fly off
once the sun gives up its battle or
just stay the night keeping the owls and
the drumming Cicadas company.
Skinks bask on the brick walls and spiders
above the bristling Juniper hedge
are suspended in expectation.
Like runny childish watercolors
the miasma of uncertainty
swims around overheated car hoods.

259
Monday, September 16, 2013

Clouds climb up their black billowing stacks
with engine pistons growling as if
to proclaim arrival. The only
party of welcome is the treetop
flurry of anxious leaves and the squall
of crows. The red soil with its blistered
dermatitis and cracked sores is too
parched to whoop it up or dance. The sun's
fright ducks its face behind scarves of dark
purple-orange—a color that calls eyes
up from their reading to gaze out the
window like timid kittens peering
from a hole cut in the side of an
overturned box. And the first splats land.

260
Tuesday, September 17, 2013

Sunlight meanders down through the bank-
side trees in their washed-out drab green leaves.
A few yellow leaves flutter aimless
whispers to the fresh mown lawn. On the
footbridge railing, an adolescent
Red Tailed Hawk stands. His venture out
from home sets him in this tense presence.
His slow neck turns as he studies the
circumference of his unblinking view.
Well shadowed Crayfish scuttle in the
creeks' trickle. Frogs dive full-length from both
banks. The Hawk's young mottled chest fluffs out.
His high boned shoulders arch. His noontime job
is to stand still and study and learn.

261
Wednesday, September 18, 2013

The now of this now is buck-solid,
bristling its antlers that claw dawn. Its
collision thuds dream's solidity
half a block down the hill. Lunging through
saplings and coarse vines, its shank wobbles
with terror against the fierce strides. With
each, the gash throbs blood. Silence holds its
breath and then exhales. The car is flung
on its side. One wheel turns. It purrs in
the gorge it cut through brush. On the porch,
chest bared, the dreamer beams a light
toward where the thud first came. A dark shape
wrestling herself up through mud, dabbing
blood with her shirt tail, is this now, now.

The Present Tense

262
Thursday, September 19, 2013

Without permission the wide window
welcomes in with gaping arms the harvest's
intruder who trails with it a
toweringly clear black sky and the
chill lies across the bed and settles in.
The city's night spills cornucopias
of ice fruit stars. It has forgotten
its dull expressway hums and loon-call
sirens. The window holds the whole cold
moon. The stars flicker inscrutable
codes of ripeness to one another
across the recesses of receding
time just as the Chorus Frogs sing their
unseen faces across the wet woods.

263
Friday, September 20, 2013

The Cypress trees fold their wings upwards
to shape gothic spires like boastful swans,
we are here. The warm dry afternoon
has put aside the last breezes from
the brief noon showers, laconically
folding them into aphorisms
in sky's blue tome and closing them shut.
In their boastful bristling, the Cypress
wings, out there, forget how to flutter.
Steaming from the small hand-glazed plate of
bunch beans and potatoes with sliced fresh
tomatoes, the aromas announce,
anew, boasting's futility. From
that now's now, this now says *I am here*.

264
Saturday, September 21, 2013

Like the equinoxes as they beam their
democratic votes of balanced light
across the year, the Viburnum makes
its return visit. The top branches
spill milk jugs of white blossoms up toward
the floating cascades of sun that stream
down through tree branches. Light splashes the
snow-soft blossoms and trickles down through
crevices of dense low foliage
into small puddles of yellow bright
warm grass. The late afternoon's clear fresh
air hangs its now on a balance. Like
this day. Like this season. Like this year.
Like this tall bush's unkempt second wind.

265
Sunday, September 22, 2013

As the TV babbles its tired
news of house fires and traffic jams, the
balcony deck beyond the sliding
glass doors bares its chest to the evening
branch-slatted shafts of light. Floundering
in a deep swoop, the adolescent
Hawk lands on the rail. His venture carries
his news this far. This near. This now.
His job is to stand still and study
and learn. His neck turns to memorize
where gables line up house roofs, where the
creek bends, where tall pines clump in the midst
of woods. Sitting six feet apart, the
day end's top news stories share a glass wall.

The Present Tense

266
Monday, September 23, 2013

Dawn postpones its curtain rise above
the tree lined stage. The tireless black of
sky plunges up into the depths of
intergalactic time. Its apex
is the moon—egg-shaped in its early
wane—and eggshell white. Its aria
shimmers coloraturas as it
climbs to its most iridescent height—
its most chastened white. A quarter sky
behind it, seamlessly, Venus's flute
follows—chaste goddess—vestal white star.
Content to watch, the stillness of air
bemoans neither night's confident slow
retreat nor dawn's certain curtain rise.

267
Tuesday, September 24, 2013

At the corner where two tall Sweetgums
have spotted themselves with yellow stars,
the flashing yellow school bus halts. Six
frolicking kids dismount and wave to
the bus. Its smoke fumes chug up the hill.
Assigned to clear the air, a wind gust
wildly flails the tree limbs. Assigned an
aerobic routine of their own, the
kids abruptly toss their backpacks to
the ground and leap to catch the falling
stars. Left hand—right hand—leap and clutch. As
if their backpacks called, they too throw
themselves onto the ground. They laugh their
summersaults and whirl their wheels of carts.

268
Friday, September 27, 2013

Yellow Jackets zoom vertically
from their hole. Gold glints on shafts of sun
are their sole presence to consciousness.
Wide enough for a paw to reach down, the
hole gapes black. The mower rumbles past
on its drive shaft. Swaths of leaf mulch stuff
its new white bag. It watches for frogs
to dive for the creek. It sees no fight
in their flight. A mandible clamps down
on the glove. Its stinger drills to the
knuckle. Another grabs the shirt and stabs
the neck. Skin behind the knee takes a
hit. The mower dives up the fresh mown
hill through the back gate. It too is flight.

269
Saturday, September 28, 2013

All morning the breeze tugs the pants legs
of the Sweetgum tree with its child hand.
It tries to keep up but faltering
it often stops in its tracks to look
up in bewilderment, searching for
assurance, longing to be lifted
and coddled. Fearful of scolding, its
tugs are timid. From time to time a
leaf is loosened and drifts like a lone
tear down across the breeze's shy face.
Morning is in no hurry to get
anywhere. Unruffled, its patience
is in no mood to scold. It coaxes
the breeze to follow. And the breeze does.

The Present Tense

270
Sunday, September 29, 2013

Dangling its broken mismatched giant
spider legs, this now sprawls out on its
gangly tomato ropes. They drape from
the wires that braced their climb to the sun.
They stare at the sprinkle of dry leaves
on the dry lawn. Their amnesia
is compete. The strong green shoots. Blank. Their
furry leaves. Blank. Their scramble up the
trellis and mustard bright blooms. Blank. The
blood blush of their large fruit and lusty
crimson juice. Blank. The lingering hard
green balls. Blank. They stare down at the gray
unblemished unresponsive after-
noon patch of lawn—with Alzheimer eyes.

271
Monday, September 30, 2013

As earth rolls the horizon up and
away from the sun's unflinching glare,
the long-armed light splashes shifting patches
of sparkling margarita lime high
across the clinking leaves at the tops
of trees. The breeze shakes variegated
pom-pom shimmy-shammies. Short skirts fluff
and shiver their pleats. As they giggle
in irrepressible voiceless
childish glee, miss and hit flutters of
spiraling unhurried leaves drift through
the dark cavernous lower branches
to hide among shadows blanketing
earth. Earth's roll moves on as the dark ascends.

October Journal

272
Tuesday, October 1, 2013

The midday breeze's chill slobbers a
puppy's tongue up and down the calves and
short shirt arms. Glasses mist up in the
fine drizzle. In a last ditch flourish,
topping the face high stalks, gecko green-
tailed okra pods stand at attention.
Wrist snap on wrist snap drops them captive
in the plastic bowl. Single-minded
Robins peck and choose through the damp mown
grass. The dove-tawny clouds lie batting
softly across the uneventful
level sky. The breeze nuzzles its cold
nose and shakes its aerosol spray of
damp clean fur. Its chill wears kindly eyes.

273
Wednesday, October 2, 2013

Bright wee roses snake through the white
upright vinyl porch rails. Sparkling in
the late morning dew, in posies at
the tips of slender green casting rods,
they dangle clusters of berry red
garnets. The wands wield whipping scourges.
Spaced like spread small fingers, the five-leafed
sprigs hide the barbs of hooks. They snare the
legs of pants. They spike right through coarse
denim weaves. They stab the flesh of thigh
and ankle. To wrench them free, thumbs take
pricks and shed small pomegranate drips.
Arrivals and departures from the
porch as proof wear surreptitious wounds.

274
Thursday, October 3, 2013

Minutes fall across the afternoon's
warm meander. Their Hickory nuts and
husks splash the wooded floor in aimless
disregard. The uneventful light
stretches spider filaments across
Boxwood shrubs where small white moths hang out
to dry. The moist dirt floor bites and stabs.
Here, no bare feet walk. Squirrels are the
business of the day. Perched on flicking
tails, their teeth saw into hulls. Minutes
count. Bounding up to park on broad limbs,
they chew the meat. Never still, here, each
moment spills down a share of shell. Moth
wing chrysanthemum petals flicker.

275
Friday, October 4, 2013

To purple Martins sailing to South
America, morning calls: *Look here.*
For you to chat and perch, phone lines stretch
above the road. Excited birds gust
black smoke up against the sun. They fall
back upon the wires in busy rows.
Beneath their mulch-machine of chatter,
sun sorts through chainsaw scraps of the wind-
felled oak. It licks at pools of spot-lit
warmth between swift cloud drift shadows. Logs
chunked like barrels lay their carcasses
rolled in the ditch. Mashed down by tires, leaves
and branches clog the street. Late morning
looks about and asks: *Satisfied now?*

276
Saturday, October 5, 2013

Rapid insistent popcorn chatter
calls school buses to their route along
the dawn-lit street and later wakes the
sun. Atop the cable, power and
phone lines from hill crest down across the
creek culvert and up the other side,
the mass of Starlings sits. Their rest stop
rest is restless. Their black wings flicker
to get back on the road. The pavement
is splotched with pit stop droppings. As sun
lifts its brow and opens its full eye,
sky is splotched with departures. By noon
bare phone lines and pavement droppings are
all that's left in the vacuum's chatter.

277
Sunday, October 6, 2013

Knowing they must not veer too far from
their ancient migration, season and
weather watch each other askance. There
is joy in pranks gone awry. While trees
protest that greens they've worn for months are
still in fashion, the morning douses
them awake with a sap-chilling mist.
It steams up car windows, it fogs up
glasses. In protest, red and ruddy-
orange shout from the wings: *what about our
grand entrances, our soliloquies
to aqua skies?* The mist wryly smiles.
And warning of mittens and coats, the
season surprises even itself.

The Present Tense

278
Monday, October 7, 2013

Because the bully wind believes it is
a fist, its boorishness does not
grasp that it's the distant tentacle
of the far off ocean hurricane.
Cowardly it waits till after dark
falls hard. Its open palm slaps car windows.
It strives to slug out eyes, to crash in
doors. When power wavers and clocks shut off,
darkness cowers. The wind's without a
plan to drive its bluster. Its haste fails
to whip up rampaging walls of rain.
Its hoarse dry wail brags. Its laughter howls.
A tree splits crashing through flocks of leaves.
Dark despair clings to the lurching light.

279
Tuesday, October 8, 2013

The school kids are boarding their buses.
Cars back out from driveways as far as
the street can see. A pause ensues. As
sunlight cascades down through it, across
fresh seeded straw covered lawns, yellow's
prophesy arrives. Here and there, like
toddlers snickering from blanket folds
or stairway banisters, the first of the
Hickories' canary leaves peek through
between the trees' gasps of bleaching green.
Overnight, weeks of future arrive
emphatically wearing the delight
that's just here now. It's mesmerizing
silent bugle blasts ring clear and gold.

280
Wednesday, October 9, 2013

Like tourists scanning grand vistas, all
day, day busies itself with the sky.
Clouds raise peaks of purple polychromes
with blooming patches of anxious gold.
They dissipate and fall apart. They
cleave the sky, one side dark with thrilling
menace; the other a bask of glaucous
blue Caríbbeán expanse. By dusk
their sweeping sheets lie in jagged shelves
with underbellies flamed in scarlet
setting rays. They watch shadows sneak
cold wind gusts on tiptoes through the yard.
Exhausted from making itself
a spectacle, day lets darkness win.

281
Thursday, October 10, 2013

Washed up from the Gulf on tropically
depressed clouds, dawn wakes beneath a slow
slapping drizzle. Weighty splats land on
leaves and struggle to tear them off. A
few soggy yellow flaps break loose. Like
the hung-over remnants of island
reggae parties, the rain beats out the
syncopations of a listless tune.
Schools of nudging bulky dolphin clouds
gyrate and bump. Between their folds, small
seams of blue crack through and then submerge.
Sternly persistent the splats' now drums
but the warmth of their rain is out of
season. Displaced far from home, it steams.

282
Friday, October 11, 2013

Like usurping siblings, air and light
join forces to conquer wind, the swirl
of clouds and the click of falling leaves
on the shed's metal roof. The Hawk on
its solo updraft is languorous
and reticent. Squirrels scratch carelessly
and shuttle off with empty jaws. All
afternoon, the alliance brooks no
treason. Light spills through air to dispense
sun's largess on trees, porch steps, parked cars,
Camellia petals that spot the ground,
bushes laced with webs and tall plumes of
Pampas Grass, while air's crispness glows with
light's artesian untouched clarity.

283
Saturday, October 12, 2013

Wraiths and nimbuses of copper light
insinuate themselves into the yards
that line the sun abandoned street. Cars
follow in close groups hurrying to
get home for late dinners. Children throw
bikes against garage walls and push each
other through back porch doors. Streetlights pop
on. Surreptitious fingers of light
slither through windows and touch kitchen
walls with glistering chrysanthemums.
The sink window rests its hands in warm
suds and takes deep breaths. In reply the
pecan tree's unhurried breath winks flecks
of light from its somnolent dry leaves.

284
Sunday, October 13, 2013

Two small Downy Woodpeckers bobble
up the up-stretched arms of the pecan
tree and tail first bobble back down.
Late afternoon overflows the back
yard. Their dapple stripes and wings are black
like gleaming coal. And like fresh snow, their
white head stripes and chests glow. Their dapples
dart and bob, while squirrels and Mourning
Doves pursue methodical patient
searches through the dry grass and fallen
leaves, and in a flash they fly away.
Senseless to pied and downy beauty,
the long arms of the pecan flutters
their drowsy song in the late-day warmth.

285
Monday, October 14, 2013

Far above the city, midnight holds
the creamy pearl of sky encompassed
in its ivory shell. Treetops below
wave their dwarfed fragility. Across
roof tops, they slowly beckon to each
other. The owl call of a train floats
though the mild air from its distant search.
The half-dried stream oozes between trees.
The train calls again. The mud banks gape
with holes, where clay mounds rise beside them
crowned with the bellows-pumping of throat-
swollen frogs. The shell-glow of midnight
choruses the wide racket and the
open window draws it wildly inside.

The Present Tense

286
Tuesday, October 15, 2013

At the corner where two tall Sweetgums
have drenched the lawn with yellow stars,
the flashing yellow school bus halts. Six
frolicking kids dismount and wave to
the bus as it scales the hill. Smoke fumes
drift behind. Blown into knee-high berms, the
leaves are crunchy soft and dry. Backpacks
stacked—jackets tossed—like puppies, the kids
frolic. Half-buried legs splash. Stretched arms
flail. Skimming the crisp sunshine with
squeals, yellow bundles erupt into
skirmishes. Choking their own laughter,
faces gulp leaves by the bucketful.
For now, now savors its entire spell.

287
Wednesday, October 16, 2013

The moon sits its half upended skiff
just above the motionless edge of
the trees. Their tops trace the jags of its
rocky shore. Above it clouds float in
dingy cream. Behind it hides the lost
horizon. Minutes measure the skiff's
inching submersion into silent
undertows. By contrast the creamy
night swarms with frog calls. Minimalist
waves of microtonal clusters pulse
from the woods across the road to those
behind the house in syncopated
riffs. Their arcs across the cool still air
pulse back and across and back across.

288
Thursday, October 17, 2013

Brushing faces and hands with almost
imperceptible fleece, rain strolls in-
to the yard. The pavement is slow to
collect small puddles across its chest.
Grass accepts a darker shade of green.
Time shifts its lens to find a different
focus but does not blink or think to
change its plans. It simply continues
its stroll letting an hour roll off
its back without a trace. As softly
as it came rain sneaks away. The fleece
gray clouds take no note it came. They watch
the western sky for clearings and their
vigilance receives its just reward.

289
Friday, October 18, 2013

Lungs do not gasp for air...they gasp in...
the crisp noon Chablis of it. The cool
cider spike of it. The butterfly
tremulous flight of it as it skims
from Aster to Aster. Mum to Mum.
Imbibing the extravagance of
it, with its prick of fresh sharp menthol,
air brushes out webs from sinuses.
Its ocean spray against pores scrubs off
the tongue and washes out the throat.
Air lifts its cool noon solidity
all the way up to the lake-still sapphire
sky. Lungs of yogis draws stillness back
down through organs and breathes it back out.

The Present Tense

290
Saturday, October 19, 2013

Shameless plastic bags blot the track-side
ditch where the wind teases the stalks of
Goldenrod. It pats their scattered locks
in place as if to ready children
for expected guests. The unruly
orphans' hair is fairytale gold.
Wind nuzzles its sun-bask warmth, ruffles
it and smoothes it again. The flowers
glare back while neighboring sprays of white
Yarrow scarcely budge. They know, like leaves
loosing color on trees, their petals'
days are numbered and wind will only
have plastic bags to kick around. For
them, now, sun and vagrant tracks suffice.

291
Sunday, October 20, 2013

Like a slow crane that wades forward and
tugs up chunks of reinforced concrete,
mid-afternoon pulls dried cucumber
vines and okra stalks. Its bent spine wades
through sun patches and shade. Its back laps
up warmth. Shadows' chills...it shivers loose.
Along the fence, pink clumps of Lady's
Thumb poke out their low nubby sprigs. Waste
mounds up above the garden wagon's
rim. It wobbles to the leaf pile out
beyond the gate. The wagon cuts a
trail through the leaf-fall grass. Like small
pink fingers, exposed Smartweeds blush. Pinks
mutter small smug impertinences.

292
Monday, October 21, 2013

The kitchen window looks up, hands deep
in breakfast suds, and steps right out to
face the tree ridge behind the yard. Drenched
in gowns of gleaming dew, Bitternut
Hickory trees vindicate their moment.
*No word for yellow good enough for
us*, they say. Other trees, like wraiths in
mist, leaves half stripped, stand back ashamed. From
every branch the Hickories glow. They call
up through the searing blue to the wedge
of ducks barking back. Letting go its
word search, the window strikes *yellow* from
its list. Inarticulateness is
good for now. The brassy leaves agree.

293
Tuesday, October 22, 2013

Venetian tromba and loud brasses
reverberate fading overtones.
Saffron chords in augmentations and
antiphonal diminutions of
gold bounce across choir-loft tops of
horizon-wide trees. With the breath-held
grip of a cresting wave riding its
setting sun tide, the buttressed aisles of
the eight arched dome glow with a stained-glass
sky. As torrid red's decrescendo
sinks, the ridge of Sycamores, Oaks and
Hickories glow sforzandos of orange
and pianissimos of yellow
shifting with each shifting stroke of light.

The Present Tense

294
Wednesday, October 23, 2013

Stillness takes over the pewter light
of evening. It sends the small weak breeze
off to bed. Leaves resolve to postpone
their erratic parachuting falls.
Silent bees jostle the Camellias
whose petals, despite their wish to join
the sibling flecks on the ground, hang on.
Like lavish webs across Juniper
shrubs, stillness casts silver white spells in
widening nets to snare the whirr and spin
of time in dusk-drenched watercolors.
It brush strokes the yard and woods as far
back as light can reach. But see, light's reach
loosens its grip. It's time to let go.

295
Thursday, October 24, 2013

Pre-dawn driveway crunch strolls down to the
street where early cars, like oars swishing through
dim shallow currents, swish through the night
fall of leaves. Solitary in the
crisp air, the stroll stalls in the center
of the road looking both uphill ways.
Each hill is splashed with pools of streetlight
light. Each a full circle. Each flecked with
glints. From the horizon, a low drone
wakes the consciousness of ears. Ahead
of it, while stillness fondles chills down
and up the watcher's bare arms and legs,
a sunlit arrow slides silver through
the seamless dark sky. The chill strolls back.

296
Friday, October 25, 2013

The Champagne evening air sparkles with
the chill of clinking crystal. It stands
erect from stooping, looks up through the
fading light and drinks a deep breath in.
The stream gorges on thick clots of orange-
gold Sweetgum leaves whose small dams back up
into pools of swirling froth. Pairs of
Dragon Flies lick the surface. Backyard
woods spread out their beds with blankets of
loose drifted leaves where slow sinking light
rustles its sheen in tipsy glints and
winks. All this here is only here. Its
fading is its here. As it sounds, the
clink goes mute. The Dragon Flies dance off.

297
Saturday, October 26, 2013

Sunlight muscles its way through the late
morning's dazzle of cold air. Returns
are mixed. With baby paw slaps, small breezes
set it back several notches. Light
pole shadows send it down a score of
chill degrees. It knows limits to strength.
Struggle persists.
Stand still beside the
brick wall. Face your east face up into
its white face. Squinch your eyes. Lean your back
back into the brick. Rest. Sun snuggles
through your shirt and warm towel wipes your
scowl. Spaced one behind the other, like
ringtones, three crows' broad arms splash across
its white brow. Their shadows leave no trace.

298
Sunday, October 27, 2013

The front porch stoop stops its watch to watch the
small mail truck trundle from one driveway
box to the next. On the opposite
side, the school bus disgorges. Kids
skitter in front of cars backed up like
a duck march down the hill. Above the
tarnished crowns of drifting yellowed leaves,
a small flock of ducks lifts cargoes of
flat feet. They cackle excitement, loop
and settle back behind the motley
canopy. A lone car's chagrin barks.
The bus lifts its flag, spews fumes at cool
air, and chugs its sunflower hulk out
of sight down the street. Cars tag behind.

299
Monday, October 28, 2013

Look at this feat! they chuck, wearing their
perky Wedgewood China whites and blues.
Flicking smart bright blades, the pair of Jays
shuffles in and out of prickly stiff
leaves, branch to branch. *Burning bush, holly
and camellia berries ripening
side by side—what cornucopias
of promise! What deliveries of
fact!* They dart past clusters of wax green
beads. *Those are for later,* they say. *Now
is now.* They tug off early blood drop
pearls. A few from that bush. A few from
this. These serve a fine midday repast,
later's unripe greens will last and last.

300
Tuesday, October 29, 2013

Beneath the press of thick gray cloud, the
light of morning sneaks like a wary
old cat about the louring stillness.
It sniffs at rotted branches shattered
up and down the street. It stares down a
shed roof hanging loose on its moorings.
It climbs about the ancient oak whose
up-ended roots claw the speechless air.
It blocks both lanes. Up the hill, flaring
dragon eyes force cars in three-way turns
to back around proceeding without
direction. Unsure whether it still
knows its way to noon, light drifts about
the half-light of its own confusion.

301
Wednesday, October 30, 2013

Owl hour's hollow gourd calls through dark's
dry Canadian breath beneath the
white apple slice of a moon. Beneath
Orion's white studded band. Beneath
Venus's piercing white eye. Air wears
the faint odor of ice. Through it the
owl's monotone cuts—intermittent
in the float of time—directionless
in the float of space. A car slips down
the hill. From driveway to driveway, its
window fires a rolled newspaper through
the dark onto each driveway. While it
spreads out yesterday across coffee
mug knees, dawn moves sure shot into now.

302
Tuesday, October 31, 2013

Falling leaves click their slow persistent
deathwatch beetle claws along the sun
porch roof. The sun's slow vermillion fall
spills amber haze along the inner
walls. Along the roofs across the road,
the amber glows. Yellow jackets flake
gold specks down and up the funnel of
air that pours from their hole in the dry
lawn up past the eaves and gutter. Breeze
is unperturbed as it nuzzles dusk's
intermittent strokes of warmth and chill.
Unperturbed the clicking minutes move
along in their knowledge that, wanting
none, they have no memories at all.

November Journal

303
Friday, November 1, 2013

The early drive time wind bursts into
angry fits. It tears off pawfuls of
Sycamore leaves and spews them down on
side road cars lined up for breaks in the
traffic. Drizzle glues them to foggy
windshields. Wipers strain to clear each clog
off. Headlights gleam on splats of lemon
paste. Like string-snapped balloons, tantrum bursts
cough up plastic bags and torn paper.
Down the embankment's stand of old trees,
an oak splits. The dead half thunders to
the marsh mud floor. Car necks jerk to look.
The widowed half shakes its burnished shawl
and flutters Willow Oak confetti.

304
Saturday, November 2, 2013

Yellow's bullish herds of grandeur tramp
through china closets of Willow Oaks
and Sycamores. They trample the hems
of the wind's skittish chill-gusting skirts.
They spin like giant mythic butterflies
flocking for their mythic southbound flights.
Beneath Hickories and Sweetgums, they
drift in billows for puppies to pounce
and roll in. The deck view looks away
and looking back, well, here, in flapping
sheets like a sail, it is, face to face,
yellow. Yellow clips a shoulder, and
like a canary swooping down with
tiny claws, yellow nests in the hair.

305
Sunday, November 3, 2013

The midnight bastinado of wind's
harsh strokes and rain's thrashings abandon
the sunrise street to wet yellow
piles. Light climbs out of the sky. It parts
the Nile flood of clouds. The street's leaf paste
is lemon slick. Early car treads crush
it into juice until four ruts—two
each side—cut through to the tarmac like
parallel black rails. Mugginess lifts
off its clammy shirt. Chills infiltrate
the air with clarity. Breath draws ice
stream zest through nostrils down to the lungs'
secret folds. Up through its throat, it lifts
tranquilities of salutation.

306
Monday, November 4, 2013

Blue is singing a clean high flute like
an ancient Egyptian goblet's blue.
Wailing aqua microtones through the
sky, wet fingers brush their crystal rims.
The eyes' inner cave walls reflect their
cerulean song the way silent
ear caves hear the inner pulse of the
jugulars beside them. The window
fails its woeful task. The sky permits
no frame to shape the view. It wants it all—
scope, height, attention. Its blue requires
eyes to breathe in synchrony. *Forget
trees and lawns and earth and be this time
with me*, it says, while silent azure holds.

307
Tuesday, November 5, 2013

Arriving for conclaves, Ladybug
ecclesiastics swarm in scarlet
gowns. They procession along wiper
blades of the mid-afternoon sun-warmed
windshield. Too intent to admire their
reflections, hushed dialogues whisper
along the rear view mirror. Solo
mediations hug the steering wheel
and sun visor. At the flick of an
index finger and thumb they spread crisp
cupped wings and bustle off, no fly-away-
home in sight. Drenched in patience, waiting
upon their misaimed flights, high wire webs
strung with booby traps, quiver with light.

308
Wednesday, November 6, 2013

A warm fog blinks its eyes but blur is all
it gets. It shucks off the blanket of
alarm clock dreams. While coffee brews, it
pads its sandals about the drifts of
cool wet leaves. The dim back yard licks toes.
Tufts of unseen breezes scuff hair and brush
calves. They call eyes upward to search
the gossamer that weaves silver through
hidden branches as if a thousand
spiders spin a shifting mesh of webs
that snare a thousand sprays of dew. The
mesh is drenched with the silver's mystery
where the half-lost rising sun lifts its
one small eye's wallflower chariness.

The Present Tense

309
Thursday, November 7, 2013

In a shower of gold, sunlight sweeps
back the heavy drapes of fog. Sweetgum
trees flare their curry saffron stars. Red
oaks tower crowns of umber flames. The
regiment of Bradford Pears strides out
in claret uniforms. Reclusive
Redbud Trees huddle whispering dry
lentil pods like eels dangling beneath
mango-peach hued leaves. The Willow Oaks'
dried mustard yellow leaves trickle down
feathers. Like kids at a holiday
toy store window, eyes can't drink up all
the dazzlement. Color goes on and
on from toe to tip. From rim to rim.

310
Friday, November 8, 2013

Picking its way through rag-tag shadows,
the setting light steps through motley trees.
It splashes yellow on receding
lower branches. Leaf glades glint like pools
of copper and amber. A lone pear
tree flares up in russet hibachi
coals. Backed by creamy sky, the distance
rings each side with black treetops. Leaving
vacancies for dark to rise from the
black ground and groping through, light stumbles,
lets go, and vanishes. On a balanced wire
between white and black, horizon clings
to afterglow's long sigh, drawing in
deep breaths of this deep now, then exhales.

311
Saturday, November 9, 2013

Reeling in midnight, the window's eyes
haul the catch down. They gasp and swallow.
Earth-lit clouds roil and streak. Between gaps
of black, diamond stabs burn through. Wind casts
nets across the trees and pulls swirling schools
of leaves down. They click and thrash fins and
scales against the balcony wall of
glass. Thumping—swarming—twirling—scraping—
cacophonies are on the move. Eyes
of the window hear through muted panes.
Rapture's score reverberates over-
tones of apprehension. The window's
eyes stab through cosmic black and back. Their
white diamonds are reeling through the night.

312
Sunday, November 10, 2013

For Marlowe
Locked up in air's glassy height and breadth,
sunlight plays laser shows on the leaves.
The still ones cling precariously
to twigs and, like yellow eyes in a
boy's spilled bag of marbles, they sparkle.
The trembling ones drool liquefactions
of silk and sequin gowns. The drifting
ones spin slowly down through pied light and
shade. The bench's black iron sits in its
warmth. Eyes adrift on light, father and
son float in wordless conversation. No
memories flit up from two score years
and three—simply the now of visit,
hike—and the this of this quietness.

313
Monday, November 11, 2013

Along the bricks of the retaining
ledge, the cat lays out blond Persian fur.
Her glottis drums private serenades
to sunbeam saunas and dazed eyelids
floating down and up. In their bath of
light, dry leaves rest in drifts along the
wall holding winter beds. Pansies wink
in gossiping circles of silent
flirtation. A chill gust cuts short late
afternoon's reverie. The cat rears
up her thighs. They stretch. Then her shoulders.
They stretch. She pussy-foots through pansy
beds and leaps across to the back porch
steps. Like an irksome cloud, she meows.

314
Tuesday, November 12, 2013

Sap delves down the safest roots to
store itself, letting leaves sever grips
that withstood hail and wind, and freeing
late ruddy browns and yellows float on
aimless drafts. For later use, it hides
its squirreled nuts of memory like
phone numbers and lines of poetry.
Remorseless it renounces brittle
twigs and barren boughs. The sun's noon glare
scans circling Hawks. They scan Starlings flocked
high on high-wires. To move the season
forward, each summons numbers to call—
lines to recall—because the precise
now that's now is not the only now.

315
Wednesday, November 13, 2013

Sundown's brief flirts with warmth snuggle in-
to moist shadow nests. Last light decamps.
Air licks at neck and ears. It watches
towering black's voiceless chatter
of far galaxies and vast nearby
suns unfurl. The now of time spreads out
in entropy and measurelessness.
Night's ancient maps and calendars are
unreadable. With forgotten names
of frost and beaver, moon glows whole. Night's
dog walker tugs a leash bereft of
names for moon, but moon. It basks in this
now's unexpected black clarity.
Orphaned, the big chalky moon basks back.

316
Thursday, November 14, 2013

The Manitoban wolf slinks down the
foothills into neighborhoods. Her pre-
dawn silence snaps frigidity's sharp
fangs into the starlit dark. She howls
record lows of *Brrrr* and *Grrrr*. She shreds
leaves from trees. In the yard, lights light their
blizzards drift against the front porch steps.
She burrows teeth into outside door
handles and porch rails. Her paw-slaps knife
at ungloved wrists and bare skin faces.
Drooling down the cheeks and icing up
the beard, their sharpness stabs blistering
helpless eyes. Her shaggy throat muffles
deep gutturals of *Grrr, Grrr* and *Brrr*.

317
Friday, November 15, 2013

Gray flannel snuggles damp siestas
down upon the tallest balding trees.
Damper mute timpani march drowsy-
lidded dreams beneath the clouds. Their half-
open eyes look down upon the team
of busy Chickadee gymnastics.
In and out the barky crevices
of Elm trees' naked arms, matinee
is in full gear. Mercurial and
shiftless, they flit and dart. Fluttering
wings chase each other branch to branch. Claws
cling upside down. With keen shafts, sun spear
stabs intrude.
Beneath leaden covers,
occluded monochromes cut them off.

318
Saturday, November 16, 2013

On kid leather pear leaves in facets
of searing light, bleached sherbet washes
of peach and lime gleam. Earth rolls up its
wide edge to douse sun's burst of lava.
Across the high abandoned sky, bleached
sherbet washes of pineapple and
raspberry unfurl ribbons and streamers.
The back yard bench wrist-flicks away nests
of dry leaves. Its gaze lifts into tints
that shift with the erratic streaks of a
vast bowl of pulpy fruit and frothy
cream. Tenderly chill floats down until
the sweater tugs to the chin and swallows
paws up inside its sleeves.
Still...now...sits.

319
Sunday, November 17, 2013

Clouds pile murky sponges, layered up,
until, as they sink to the trees, their
weight hides the sky. Parched and shriveled leaves
dangle on thin claws. Weariness aches
to let go. They long to fall. Clouds soak
up all the damp they can and slowly
wring it out. Noon's muggy chill dribbles
through the dense air then gathers force. Its
vertical determination wins
out. Pellets splat the tired leaves. Glad for
an excuse, their claws snap. Last leaves tear
loose. Afternoon drives down in hoards till
black trunks stand alone on the roadside.
Car brakes squeal and skid the leaf-sleek hill.

320
Monday, November 18, 2013

Night crests and swells. Boney shadows thrash
the street-lit pavement. Scurrying clouds
loom then flatten as the moon tosses
on ball-bouncing waves. While the shadows
splash the window glass, vinyl siding
creaks like bulkheads of old boats. Night is
its own repeating tempest of a
dream that hungers for the balm of snow
that does not come. A crash squints awake
to face the two o'clock hands, but the
submerging dream returns full force. As
dawn drifts in on quite ripples of
soft light, a log-sized limb dangles wedged
into the tree's crotch above the porch.

321
Tuesday, November 19, 2013

Like the silent loping of a deer
as it emerges out of shadows,
passes and subsides in the distance,
beneath the ripe gold of the full moon
a solo runner glides down the street.
His tireless legs glow white and lithe in
washes of lunar clarity. His
white gloved hands piston-pump the frost cleaned
air. Beneath his hood, breath clouds spurt from
his thrumming oxygen-flushed heart. His
loping stride passes the house. Without
a shift of gear, his body leans as
he glides up the steep hill.
The morning
paper dangles from the watching hand.

322
Wednesday, November 20, 2013

Between sparseness of leaves, afternoon's
trees, satiny with slow drizzle, nap
in rust-bronze gowns. They draw window's gaze
far into the freshness that now is
their new distance. In the hush that falls
after frantic crow caws cease, they dream
of black trunks parading in legions
out into extravagant sunsets.
They dream of barren branch tops crowned with
lime green bonnets of bright Mistletoe.
They dream of standing guard in the light
of a full and icy moon. They dream
of days whose great events are snugness
in hibernation and deep warm roots.

323
Thursday, November 21, 2013

As light packs up to sail west, the
air tastes chilly cider residue.
On the ledge above the tired rake,
the few last sips at the bottom of
the thick mug fill the mouth and linger
happily. They scarcely notice how
alone they are. All day the palate
is busy with the herby dryness
of leaves. The mouth imbibes gulps—all day—
of cold air spiked with dust. Now air takes
in, with each waning sip, pristine breaths
of vanishing light and holds their bright
bouquet. Scattering light's soft ashes
across still dark waters, air exhales.

324
Friday, November 22, 2013

Late morning unsnaps its jacket and
slips its gloves off. It strolls down the hill.
The shrinking shadows strive to change its
mind. It crosses the slender bridge and
the sun catches up. In their renewed
camaraderie they peer up at the
house on the hill, its puppet lanky
trees, dried azalea bushes, roses
shrunken like locust hulls. Settling down
on the porch swing, their conversation
quickens, glugs the last of the coffee,
sets the cup down and lays back its head.
Closed eyes drift, with shirt-front bared, in the
warm haze of blood pink lids. And noon waits.

325
Saturday, November 23, 2013

Resigned to be bare patches of cold
clay where fallen leaves are scuffed aside,
afternoon crawls parched and impotent.
It mumbles through circle on circle
of prayer beads whose repeats transform time
to timelessness. It kneels and looks down
on the stream whose leaf clogged pools are glass.
Their lit icons flicker in the shade
of the bank. Unmoving, afternoon
succumbs to a trance. Unmoving, the
stream stares back. From carcasses of trees
in distant wetlands, unnoticed crows
caw and scold the ears' inner edge but
they are tuned to hear silence only.

326
Sunday, November 24, 2013

Sunrise glares down into the eyes of
creeping yellow busses. It swaggers
and nags: *stomp your feet and roll your hands
up inside your shirt.* It blows cold gusts
and sniggers. It says: *Stretch each minute
out its full length, like leathery tired
bubble gum.* Light's impertinence drowns
out chattering the mobs of Starlings
that rise up from and fall back upon
barren oaks, transmogrifying their
wings into ice-like silver darts. Cowed
and bludgeoned, the chill morning staggers
toward a day that it might want to be.
I'm not done yet, sun-glare boasts, slow down.

327
Monday, November 25, 2013

With insults upon indignities,
heads tuck down into the clavicle
hoping it sprouts a sheltering wing.
Slants of pettifogging rain mete out
miniature scourges. Cold saliva
spews miniature curses. Wind joins
forces in its heedless glee. Scrunched down
inside its drudgery, the trudging
face celebrates only its push all
the way to the back yard gate. On the
other side, the wake of the huge felled
tree is a mud splash along the length
of the fence. Mute terror of the crash
quivers across early afternoon.

328
Tuesday, November 26, 2013

An ice starched breeze flaps at day's cold start.
Children at the school bus corner roll
cold hands up inside their shirts. Their dads'
hunker under hoodies to talk to
ear phone phones. The breeze ignores them. Its
resolve herds dry leaves into curbside
furrows. It catches plastic shopping
bags and, like half deflated balloons,
sweeps them up to snag bare branches. It
chases squirrels around underbrush
in frantic searches for Hickory nuts.
The bus grinds up. It grinds away. As
dads stagger to their porches, the breeze
slaps their backs with its bad joke punch line.

329
Wednesday, November 27, 2013

While cold's persistence officiates,
afternoon's amnesia sweeps away
the dinge of clouds. Sundown plays suites of
madrigals on pianissimo
recorders. Counterpoints weave off-beats
at low registers. Modulations
melt. Descant sherbets—treble creams—drops
of lemon tenors—contra basses
in their azure barkings—and dancing
at the upper edges, small piquant
sopranino tangerines. To keep
the entire contrivance going, cold
air controls a steady breath...breathes...and
breathes...and breathes...against cadential dark.

330
Thursday, November 28, 2013

Striking from the southern nether-side,
sunlight falls slant. Ivy columns flow
up the barren oaks. In shimmering
emerald schists, they trill the light. Northern
sides swaddle folds and crevices of
moss green granite. With even-handed straight-
edge, compass and protractor, slants cut
columns across barren yards. They lie
in starkly flat parallels of black.
Mindless of boundaries, they slice straight
across bare flower beds and raked leaf mounds.
Imperceptibly creeping forward
their rigid dials, early afternoon
sits in horizon-wide rail-straight stripes.

331
Friday, November 29, 2013

The mower drives a circuitous
trench through the leaf-drifted yard and hauls
mulch to its mound out back. Sharply, now
eroticism's wind begins its
slow burn. Despite chill, the worn coat pulls
off and drapes the gate. Wind nibbles nape—
cheek—wrists. Sun's morning slant glares. It pays
no heed to the seduction of the
sharp cold darts. Circuit follows circuit,
haul follows haul. The wind's chores have no
end in sight; its back and shoulders do
not tire. Meanwhile leaf-damp's slow tingle
licks through socks and fondles toes. Forlorn
the coat on the gate flaps with each gust.

332
Saturday, November 30, 2013

Grid-bound, weary and home-hungry, dusk
is locked in an indolence of time.
Its aftermath of light glides between
stark trees. It inches out over the
shaggy blanket of bare lots with
weeds broke off, and grass beat down to straw.
Caution steps out on skittish doe hooves
like apparitions in the gloaming,
one—now two—now imperceptibly
—at least—ten—grazing with alert ears,
cocked and twitching at the line of cars.
Slowing to a near full stop, fading
light strains to look, while, to avoid lurch
and crash, it strains against breathless dread.

December Journal

333
Sunday, December 1, 2013

The night's dim clouds float on the city's
glow. Like upended scorpions and
tarantulas, trees stretch from all sides
with skeleton tentacles and claws.
Their convocation speaks in tongues of
silence. Their gestures are as subtle
as a twinge. They deliberate. They
reach consensus. Stars are banned. Moon must
hide. Only one long train is allowed
to croon its strained call to each crossing
street as it creeps its tortoise hulk down
the track of the ear's horizon. Wrapped
in the bath robe, ears stand immersed
in the window's unyielding display.

334
Monday, December 2, 2013

Large enough to be a plowed corn patch
and garden, the neighbor's vacant house
stretches its backyard out like a beach
beneath the cool bright sun. Afternoon
is a stretch of hardscrabble dry grass
and windblown furrows of dead leaves. From
the barren woods at the far back, like
wraiths out of nowhere, drift three does. Three
more follow. Their necks curve into the
stubble. As the snapshot shoots the next
quick-shutter shot, fifteen deer graze in
a dream's slow motion. Heads lift. Ears flick
and twist. Necks bend back down. Sunlight glows
on the caramel glaze of tan backs.

335
Tuesday, December 3, 2013

The fog presses through the cold swamp of
morning and eventually takes on,
like an unfamiliar rival, the
early afternoon's occluded light.
With its beams aimed low, each car crawls past
the other cars like old men on their
knees with flashlights quivering as they
look for pills that rolled beneath their beds.
Tree branches loom up over the road
with the menace of prehistoric
reptilian bones. But the fog digs
in its heels and hunkers down for the
few remaining hours till nightfall.

336
Wednesday, December 4, 2013

Sun's exuberant rush up the sky
sweeps off shadows. The polish of fresh
light sizzles icy mica flakes on
lawns. Exhaling from the Juniper
hedge, a tang of morning sweetness wafts
across the shivery air. Like a
bundled up gnome, a child bobbles
up the curb to the hilltop stop sign.
Sheen of frost like sugar glazes the
dry grass. A second house, a second
child bobbles out. And a third. And two
more. As it swaggers up the distant crest,
boxy and loud, eight gnomes wave to the
mustard gold troll to come scoop them up.

337
Thursday, December 5, 2013

Veiled in its midmorning aster blue
scarf with angora white wool patches,
sky spreads a fjord and glacier bay
with bobbing skiffs. The slowly drifting
eastern sun taps its wand with bands of
butterfly yellow on cloud edge here
or cloud edge opposite. As if the
hour were as motionless as they are,
four deer forget skittishness and nip
grass tufts on the creek bank. Serving ice
water in a crystal goblet, the
slow stream in the creek bottom's creases
of mud faintly chugs and glitters.
Above the trees, clouds sail out the bay.

338
Friday, December 6, 2013

With a Wren's persistence at a patch
of dry grass, the sun pecks doggedly
at the undersides of ice frozen
on chandelier limbs. In clandestine
caves of starless dark, sleet of evening's
drive-time rain froze solid. Half a day
away, ice clings undaunted by the
glaring sun's affronts and its brazen
onslaughts. Persistence hails its triumph.
Outbreaks of glee loosen ice chunks to
slip off. Their silver clatters down to
bare grass's midday patch, glistering
like the blast from a shattered windshield.
Ice shards drop. Sun licks. Ice drops. Sun licks.

339
Saturday, December 7, 2013

Grass patches hibernate in spongy
clay. They sidelong glance around edges
of bulky house shadows to find
early bands of flat low distant sun
then snuggle back in their cool damp nests.
Mocha slicks of clay encroach the down-
trod path from porch to compost bin. They
relish splashed pants legs and gummed up shoes.
Splotched along it, the path tells tale-signs
of night's marauder: corn cob, orange peel,
moldy bread. Night hides ambidextrous
paws and bandit mask. Dawn holds deeds of
darkness up to the glare of day and
nibbles at the shadows' sharp edges.

340
Sunday, December 8, 2013

Unperturbed by dreams and cold night air,
Jupiter, the moon's glowing crescent
scythe, and Mars, climb ladder rungs up the
midnight sky. The blanket cave snuggles
out night's cold air. Unperturbed by dreams,
marauder paws wedge up the curbside
recycle lid. Head-first inside, claws
shred white plastic bags. Crash and jangle.
Wine bottles smash splinters of carnage.
Vomited across the driveway, reek
rancid bean cans and ice-cream cartons.
Unperturbed by night's cave-warm sleep, with
a surgeon's fastidious deftness,
bandit hands lift morsels to their lips.

341
Monday, December 9, 2013

The deck swing in its nook imbibes late
morning sun. Its now is a puff soft
island-scape of somnolent snowy
clouds. Its here sways in mulled cider and
spice spiked air. Its light bleeds through squinted
lids in drowsy pulses and gentle
ruby stabs. Its warmth elongates cat-
stretching legs that rock like cradles on
their pivot heels. Sipping down quaffs of
now, its body yawns.
The Wren, busy
in her alternate now, flickers down
from the pecan branch. From the deck rail,
her stillness surveys the straw dry lawn.
Plop. She stains the rail with a dollop.

342
Tuesday, December 10, 2013

In spots of blushing time, Camellias
lay modest pink stars along the stiff
dark leaves. A solitary stingless
bee snuggles in the petal folds. It
nurses the creamy yellow pollen.
With motionless caresses, it basks
in suckling stupor. Warmth drizzles
soft breaths on the bush's leathery
stiff leaves. In embarrassment, its blush
absorbs a solipsistic present
tense. Bush, blossom and bee—in their genes—
see the aberrance that this warmth is.
They know a cloudless noon suckles well
too. With frost on grass, they know it will.

343
Wednesday, December 11, 2013

The sky clears its mind of day-lit thoughts
and opens wide to rush the moon in.
Unapologetic cascades of
noiseless light etch eaves and walls, in
parallelograms on lawn on lawn,
black and gray, and draws utility
poles and their shadows with angles lined
by compasses and straight edges all
the way down the street's vanishing point
as if ideas had shapes. But watch.
The noiselessness is just now not here.
An owl pencils its plaint across the
ears like the puff from a Spanish fan.
The moment shifts on. And puffs again.

344
Thursday, December 12, 2013

The wind rolls in on shrieking rails and
sweeps late morning's low dank clouds ahead.
Chill climbs down into the silent air
that follows now and welcomes growling
school buses that stop to flag down cars
searching out their driveways to creep home.
Step into this evening air—this now.
Taste inexplicable dawn cries of
back yard Vietnamese Roosters from
around the corner. Falsetto bites
the warm tongue. The palette is tickled
as the chilled cork is popped and the air's
bouquet of feather-fine bristles stings
up into the face's cavities.

345
Friday, December 13, 2013

With a wheelchair's stoic labor up
an incline, afternoon spends its small
daylight change. It drifts a few slow red
oak leaves as they let go tired
grips. Like gravel, they click along the
shed roof metal. Three squirrels claw at
hoard holes in the bare lawn. They come up
dry. They scamper to new spots and try
again. And again. In a splotch of
direct sun, the next door dog naps on
her chain tightly coiling herself
with her tail over her nose. The
change is spent. The splotch dries up. With plans
to stay the good night, shadows crawl in.

346
Saturday, December 14, 2013

The drab gray chill of sunless sunrise
eases into drab gray morning. Morning
incrementally eases degree
upon degree until noon's dawn of
thinning cloud. Noon exhales deep gulps of
warmer air. The neighbor's dog pricks her
ears at a siren pummeling toward
a fire across the woods and lifts her
throat in a wolf wail. Startled squirrels
digging holes in the dry lawn bound at
trees and scurry up. Afternoon ticks
up another handful of degrees.
The broad white sky concurs and says, *A
sweater's quite enough for evening walks.*

347
Sunday, December 15, 2013

Morning wakes fitfully from sultry
dreams. Its sleep is overheated as
it sloughs off the unneeded blankets.
Dank with restless odors, it squints its
eyes out into the murky dank mist
where intermittent street lights diffuse
gray beams toward each other like lone calls
of owls. Sunlight is tentative and
takes its time. Morning is in no haste
to relinquish air's surprise. Thawing
gurgles in fetid unraked leaves and
makes small swamps beneath indefinite
shapes of trees. Thawing exhales a gray
halitosis right in morning's face.

348
Monday, December 16, 2013

The transom balcony window snakes
eyes along the chilled tawny milkish
creek as its serpent spine winds beneath
the black wet trees. Branches drip random
ripples. Their chill reaches up to the
dwindling light of low clouds. They weigh down
with dark fog as night creeps in. Out of
the corner of the window's eye, on
the creek bank, a pair of bedraggled
squirrels zips up the lofty oak. Its
bare branches grip their leafy burrow.
They disappear. The blinds slide shut their
slats. Waving a pendulum through the
wide transom, the nest nods a black blotch.

349
Tuesday, December 17, 2013

Silver fog slinks out of the dense night
in her seven motionless silken
veils. She fills the intestacies of
the trees and the houses with gentle
motionless caresses. She brushes
against black ivy vines and window
panes. Motionlessly they return each
silver blush. As each veil drops away,
a brighter silver sways its open
arms until the seventh falls. Just now—
opaque florescence chimes silent bells
motionlessly from hunched down driveway
cars and upstairs blackened window glass
back through the fogbound vanishing woods.

350
Wednesday, December 18, 2013

Beneath the shelf of clouds, darkness wakes
its appetite. The pre-dawn air is
lemon sherbet crisp. The tongue wraps it
up within its breath. It savors the
long draft ride down the wind pipe to fill
the lungs with sassy tang. The sun hangs
back in the wings waiting to bring on
the main course. It tosses small puffs of
raspberry pink chilled shrimps up against
the underside of clouds as a tease
again the palate. The palate stands
solitary in the presence of
its naked consciousness. Taste and breath,
tongue and lung are fused as one organ.

351
Thursday, December 19, 2013

Midmorning sneaks calm pools of light in
between abrasive chilly breezes
and drops them where sun patches stand still.
The breezes flip ivy leaves upside down
on tree trunks. Theirs is a tireless green
whose knotted twines mesh mercilessly.
The pools swim their calms with haloes of
gnats that lift swirling plumes, dizzily
suspending themselves inside the air,
then, as if air dropped out its bottom,
plummet *en masse* toward dead grass like a
fumbling diver. The last moment and
morning catches its breath to push the
gnats spinning helix back toward the sun.

352
Friday, December 20, 2013

Beneath piles of pillowing dirt gray
clouds, abrasively mid-afternoon
sneaks in with stabs of cold on wrists and
cheeks. On their rock-firm roots in stoic
rigidness, trees withstand the buffets.
Their leafless spires don't waver. They don't
snap. Rude and unpredictable as
a butting goat, the bastinado
wind does not relent. Its traceless stealth
is as cold as any stone. Numbness
starts imperceptibly and blow by
blow insinuates its depth. The clouds
hang their shameless drooping shaggy locks.
They catch snarls in spiny tops of trees.

353
Saturday, December 21, 2013

Cold dribbles from shed eaves. Mist fizzes
soda spray. In front of the open
door, barren packed clay slides on congealed
lard. Boxes of sorted discarded books
sponge up the wet grass. As it plods through
slow chores, strong early afternoon tea
puffs clouds from the mug parked on the ledge.
Its numb fingers scoop mouse nests from box
bottoms. They drop their silk mesh in the wide
black trash bag. They sweep out mounds of nut
shells and peppercorn turds. They pull down webs.
Swaying and tapping against the door,
Nandina Berries spark ruby coals.
Wet weight hangs low as solstice light fades.

354
Sunday, December 22, 2013

The sunlight drifts its horizontal
flatness between motionless landlocked
trees like river froth. Only,
holly and Oregon Grapes are lapped
with stony agate and dark jade sheens.
The flatness floats across the granite
gray of roofs, the asphalt glint of streets.
Standing in the open doorway, a
held breath cannot hold itself for long,
but horizontals hold all the light
of day till duskily they exhale.
Day turns around. Like slow ship rudders,
long flat sunlight slowly wheels shadows
around from due west past north to east.

355
Monday, December 23, 2013

The temperature puts on its poker-
face sometime during the night. As it
lowers expectations one degree
at a time, it neither grimaces
nor smiles. Glass-hard ice oozes out of
night's drizzle and fog to spread flawless
glaze on car windows and doors sealed tight.
The surreptitious pavement wears a
layer of hard black surprises. The steps
down from back yard decks shuffle and deal
a losing hand, and gradually as
daylight grows milkier, the fog plays
a winning trump card. Thick as sour cream
it teaches wheels to spin and burn tires.

356
Tuesday, December 24, 2013

The frosty stalks of dried Cornflowers
whistle in their skittish chickadee
way calling sunlight back to crystal
specks. But it has crawled low between sheds
and slender trees that stand like cardboard
props along the rear horizon of
a child's wobbling diorama. Light
lies along the ground wearing a gray
crepuscular train that slowly trails
long behind the vanished sun's dark red
gown. Fresh with frost, stalks stand alone in
the dimming forestage light and drama's
stoic frieze. Like a child's forgotten
lines, they relinquish their wish to call.

357
Wednesday, December 25, 2013

The stripped tree branches and the falling
snow fleece spin receding counterpoints
in the silent boys choir cathedral
serenity. Their resonances
reverberate their soundless double
paths deep into woods where eyes seek trails.
Ears hold their peace. The air is light with
light. The branches wave black wands, chopsticks
and batons. Their rhythms mesmerize.
The snowflake melismata fall and
lift with the agility of pure
soprano pre-pubescence. Double
moving paths weave their now into each
next new now as all time always does.

358
Thursday, December 26, 2013

The backyard gentle sift of white spreads
wide its eager eyes. Bird claw needle
point stitches track the ends and odds of
yesterday's handfuls of flung out seeds.
Sitting atop its low eastern perch
of barren trees, sun's brash reveille
jerks up its warning: *Take a good look
now. I'm set to clear it all away
Let syrupy puddles flow.* And sure
enough, claw by claw, the tracks dissolve.
Only the shade behind the shed stakes
out a small defiance. Sun does not
see this hidden impertinence. As
minutes melt one to the next, it does.

359
Friday, December 27, 2013

Rain slants its thin silky veils one
behind the next across the sprawl of
helpless noon. The sheets recede into
distant density. The smothered light
is helpless gray. A car snakes spotlight
eyes down the hill. It sprays a wake of
gritty gruel. Clutching helplessly, the
beams stretch flailing tentacles. On the
culvert crossing, puddling yanks the beams
headlong down into the marshy lawn.
Cowering in shame on spinning tires, the
car grinds out backwards. The tentacle
beams climb the hill opposite. Two deep
gashes in the grass gag with water.

360
Saturday, December 28, 2013

Rain drives fire hose plateaus of cloud
up the ramshackle eastern sky. Bold
black trees march into the trombone blare
of late afternoon sun. The towering
wall of Cypress spires shimmers diamonds.
The Holly hedge flecks pomegranate
garnets. The pavement exhales chilly
small whiffs of steaming tea. Lawn's matted
fur is otter slick. Its ruts gleams oil
and white. As if they chipped down from the
afterbirth blue sky, five Jays pluck through
the mud. Like wands, blue, red, diamonds and
black chase all shades of gray packing. They
congratulate each other, *Job done.*

361
Sunday, December 29, 2013

Fog slowly writhes about in its pre-
dawn miasma. Erasing trees and
houses, dark smothers light refracted
through the treacherous damp. Slowly out
of leafless tall bushes, chill-sharpened
tentacles seethe. Trees walk their bones in
and out of gloom. Haloed in dark webs,
branches claw through light's shifting body.
They emerge and fade. Engorged with dark,
fog mutters a silent colorless
white glow. They are variants of each
other in this hushed present's presence:
synonyms...light means dark means light...and
oxymorons...neither's opposite.

362
Monday, December 30, 2013

Rain's all day curtains shimmer cold gray
satin between the kitchen window and the dark
tweed leafless trees. Beyond their forlorn
herring bone bark, the horizon's charcoal
ashy light floats tin tint and washed out
cinemátográphs. Resigned to their
monochrome gruel, their sole spice is
yellow Turmeric's crisply layered
Hornbeam frocks. Unlike the helpless green
chokeholds of ivy ropes on old oaks,
their persistence entices the wet
uncertain light to burnish them as
far as the kitchen window sees. From
behind, its oven basks in warm sage.

363
Tuesday, December 31, 2013

Morning wakes with wide ears cocked up at
reverberations of its present
tense. Tense with the shimmering presence
of its hollow blare, the train wails
along ears' vanishing point. In the
crackly crisp air, wind chimes jingle small
random swirls of climbing overtones.
Horizon echoes proximity.
Proximity calls horizon back.
Up through its tunnel of filament
nerves, ears swirl, as they score blots across
the yard from the sun's long shadows' chimes.
Nerves hum air's cold plaint. Snapping a shot...
its shot...now... now flits across the brain.

Poems from this book have appeared in the following print and online publications: *The Axe Factory. The Birds We Piled Loosely. Blast Furnace. The Camel Saloon. Charlotte Viewpoint: Metropolitan Ideas & Art. Corvus Review. Eunoia Review. Drunk in a Midnight Choir. Drunk Monkeys. Grey Sparrow Journal. Iodine Poetry Journal. Indiana Voice Journal. Jellyfish Whispers. The LABLETTER. Leaves of Ink: Poetry Without Limits. Leveler. Linden Avenue Literary Journal. Mad Swirl: A Creative Outlet. Nine Mile: Art & Literary Magazine. Off The Coast. Peacock Journal. Peeking Cat Poetry. The Penmen Review: Southern New Hampshire University's Online Journal for Creative Writers. Pif Magazine. Pinyon Review: Celebrating The Arts & Sciences. Plum Tree Tavern. Poydras Review. Pyrokinection: Where Words Come to Burn. River Poets Journal. San Pedro River Review. Scarlet Leaf Review. The Tower Journal. Ucity Review. Wilderness House Literary Review. Ygdrasil: A Journal of the Poetic Arts.*

And in these print anthologies: *Element(ary) My Dear. The Four Seasons. Lost in Orange. Peacock Journal Anthology: Beauty First.*

Made in the USA
Middletown, DE
24 July 2018